Draw the Line

Jeff Traylor, the Gilmer Buckeyes,
and a Season Deep in the
Heart of East Texas

Hunter Taylor

Foreword by
Jeff Traylor

Hunter Taylor

Draw the Line:

Jeff Traylor, the Gilmer Buckeyes, and a Season Deep in the Heart of East Texas

ISBN (Print Edition): 978-1-66783-146-6

ISBN (eBook Edition): 978-1-66783-147-3

© 2022 Hunter Taylor. All rights reserved. No part of this publication may be reproduced, distributed, or transmitted in any form or by any means, including photocopying, recording, or other electronic or mechanical methods, without the prior written permission of Hunter Taylor, except in the case of brief quotations embodied in critical reviews and certain other noncommercial uses permitted by copyright law.

To my wife, Brittany
Home is wherever you are

"Beyond high school one can no longer believe in football. One can work at it, emotionally as well as physically, but faith in its full meaning is bound to be questioned, if not altogether abandoned."

Geoff Winningham

Foreword

When Hunter first told me about this project and the heart behind it, I immediately told him, "Just let me know how I can help."

You see, high school football in East Texas is different. It's almost religious in the way people from this region follow their teams, their coaches, and their kids; and their loyalty lasts long after each team member's time on the field is over. In fact, I think that might just be my favorite thing about this area. If you're one of theirs, they'll back you for life. My career is evidence of that.

I grew up in East Texas, I played ball in East Texas, and I was fortunate to learn how to be a coach right here in East Texas. In my opinion, it is the mecca for high school football and high school coaching, and I'm so proud to be a part of its history.

It's also a place where coaches matter. In these small, country towns, families will entrust their kids to the school's coaches to teach them how to be a young man or young woman. It's one of the greatest partnerships that still exists in education and society, and this story offers a glimpse into how many lives have been changed by the miraculous work of high school coaches.

Oh, and there's also some pretty good ball in this area of the state, too. Dating back to players and teams like Earl Campbell, Billy Sims, and the great Big Sandy and Daingerfield teams of the 70s and 80s, this region has a rich history of producing some of the best athletes in the world, and this book will show you just how much influence this region has had on the game of football on all levels, and continues to have today. I'm especially honored that some of my former players, teams, and friendly rivals are included in it.

Finally, I have had a friendship with Hunter for almost ten years now, and one of the things I always admired about him was the level of care and integrity he puts into anything he does. He's a fellow East Texan, a former high school coach himself, and a high school coach's son. I think he nailed this story, and I'm so proud of him.

Not only will this book give you a keen sense of the rich history of football in East Texas, it will also give you examples on how to lead. Men like Danny Long, Matt Turner, and Alan Metzel made me a better man and a coach, not just because of how they taught the game, but how they lived their lives. I'm so excited for you to get to know them and several others through these accounts.

--Jeff Traylor

Table of Contents

Introduction	1
Chapter 1: A Game of Inches	7
Chapter 2: Birthplace of the Yamboree	21
Chapter 3: The Ultimate Slogan	29
Chapter 4: The Marshall Legacy	43
Chapter 5: The Transfer	61
Chapter 6: The Proving Ground	75
Chapter 7: Little Brothers	93
Chapter 8: PRIDE	115
Chapter 9: The Passing Game	133
Chapter 10: Who's the BEAST?	153
Chapter 11: Hot Streak	171
Chapter 12: Championship Culture	187
Chapter 13: Jerry World	207
Chapter 14: #bEASTtexas	221

Chapter 15: #JeffTraylorForHeadCoach   243

Epilogue   265

Introduction

It's 4 p.m. on the dot when a whistle alerts the entire room that it's time for the team meeting to begin. "Lock in," says head coach Matt Turner.

There are still three and a half hours until kickoff for the Gilmer Buckeyes, but their gameday process starts now. The team is right in the middle of their 2018 district season, and they are scheduled to line up against the defending state champions, the Pleasant Grove Hawks, later that night. The entire varsity roster is in the Gilmer athletic fieldhouse's film room, seated with eyes glued to the front of the room. They're comfortable but focused.

In a time period where teenagers are characterized by having short attention spans, this particular team seeks to defy the norm.

The first assistant coach walks to the front of the room. Sporting black Buckeye sweats and a scruffy beard, he confidently offers three reminders for his responsibility area on Gilmer's punt coverage. No one else is talking. No one else is even moving.

The next assistant coach then does the same thing, walking to the front of the room, again offering three more points that cover a different aspect of their special teams coverage. Three more do the same thing. Turner is standing at the back of the room where no one else can see him. With each person delivering their content reminders, he rocks back and forth from the balls of his feet to his heels. He even mouths in silence the exact same instructions that are given by each special teams coach. No one knows more about the intricacies of the game and this team than him, but he wants each assistant to have a level of autonomy and expertise before the team.

Once the five special teams coaches are finished delivering their reminders, Turner returns to the front of the room.

He then tells the players thank you for their undivided attention before listing off the next procedures that will guide them all the way until kickoff at 7:30 p.m.

Turner is a walking contradiction of sorts. The respect he is given from everyone in the room shows how commanding of a presence he has, but he demonstrates more kindness and gratitude in a five-minute speech than most "alpha" leaders do in an entire week.

Once his instructions are over, he then asks the players to leave the room, so the training staff can set up for the pre-game meal, but before he does, he points out the special guests in the room that are not part of the football program.

"Men, before you leave the room, please go by and introduce yourself and tell them how glad we are that they're here," said Turner.

Every single player follows the sage coach's instructions, also making it a point to offer eye contact and a firm handshake. It's obvious they have been taught this.

Once the meal tables have been set up, the lines start to form on each side, and the head trainer, Steve York, fires up a video on the projector.

As the players are enjoying their sandwich and chips, laughter starts erupting once they see the homemade movie. Different faces of popular assistant coaches have been cropped over the actors of a "buddy-cop" movie, and the players can't get enough of it. It's time to relax and enjoy everyone's company right now, and York has accomplished the objective.

After the film ends, Turner re-emerges at the front of the room. It's quiet again, and he introduces the Bible verse of the week that is displayed on the whiteboard. He then asks offensive coordinator and local pastor, Alan Metzel, to come up for the pre-game chapel.

It's clear by how they introduce one another that Metzel and Turner share a deep amount of respect, and in an ironic way both men showcase a similar demeanor, one that models both kindness and toughness.

Metzel begins by praising York and the training staff for the work they did to create a fun video and set up the meal. He then recognizes each member of the coaching staff by name for the great work they've collectively done to prepare the players for competition. His words are sincere, yet succinct, delivered to a staff and players who clearly love and respect him.

Metzel then grabs a black dry erase marker and begins sketching the outline of a mountain on the whiteboard. At certain points in the outline's edges, he lists off season markers divided into three phases. There was pre-district play with all of the opponents listed, there was district play with all of the opponents listed, and then finally there was the upcoming playoff bracket. Then, at the top of the mountain, he draws a flag with the words, "Become the men God has called us to be!"

Metzel briefly describes each phase, and how all of their actions are designed to accomplish these phases, ultimately with the goal of becoming godly men.

Finally, he finishes by telling them, "You're ready. I love you. God loves you. Now, let's go demonstrate the greatest love story on the field."

Turner then comes behind his friend and colleague with the final words to the team, "Let's go, men."

***

In a region like East Texas, scenes like this help tell its story. It's a land of tough, committed, resilient, hard-working people who love and take care of each other, and the area's coaches are oftentimes the ones who do the best job of molding each successive generation.

There's also a humility to this area. It's not flashy or self-promoting like some of the state's larger cities. It just gets the job done, goes home, and wakes up and does it again.

That's probably why most people have never heard of coaches like Matt Turner or Alan Metzel, and honestly, they probably like it that way. They represent an ethos that is firmly embedded in so many of these small towns: they just want to be faithful with what they've been given.

Their story, representative of so many other ones, is not only the story of teams, players, and schools. It's the story of a region.

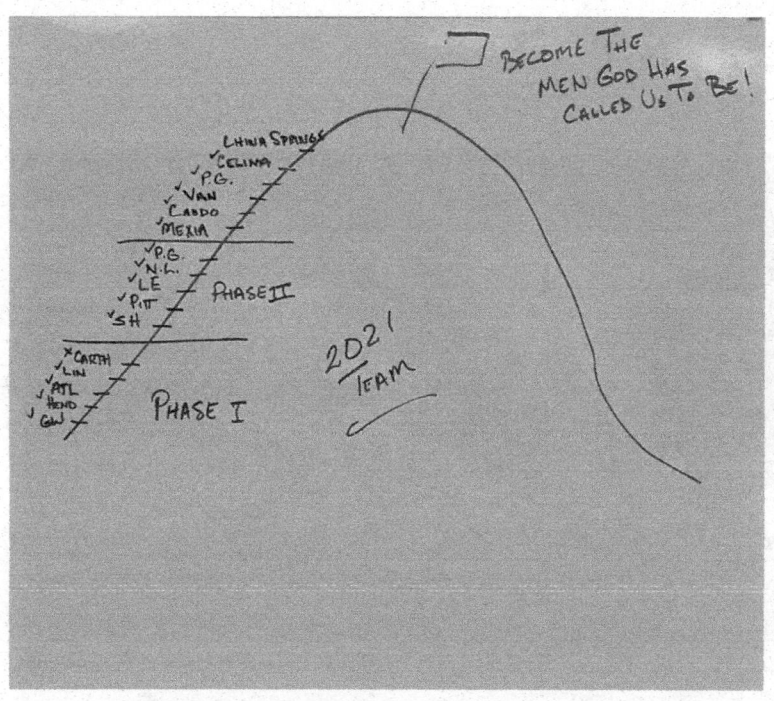

Coach Alan Metzel's sketch of "The Mountain" on his team's whiteboard in Gilmer's athletic fieldhouse. (Courtesy of Alan Metzel)

Gladewater's Daylon Mack gets tackled by a group of Buckeye defenders in their playoff game at Lobo Stadium. The game drew an estimated crowd of 12,000 spectators. (Courtesy of Ruel Felipe)

"We're about to win this whole thing."
--Jeff Traylor

Chapter 1: A Game of Inches

You could have heard a pin drop in Longview's Lobo Stadium.

Twelve thousand hushed fans huddled together in the November cold watched as referees brought out the chains. One stretched the iron links to their limit while the other leaned over to measure the seemingly imperceptible distance between a yard marker and the nose of a football.

On the previous play, Jackson Sikes of the Gilmer Buckeyes—all 180 pounds of him—had dove at the legs of Daylon Mack, star fullback for the Gladewater Bears. Mack, who weighed 300 pounds and ran a 4.9 40-yard dash, was on the radar of college football coaches across the country.

Before Sikes's maneuver, Gladewater had had the ball on the Gilmer 19-yard line, leading 35-33, and they'd opted to go for a first down and put the game out of reach rather than kicking a field goal on fourth and two. The call was fullback dive, a simple play. It had worked for at least two yards nearly the entire game.

Everyone in the stadium knew who was getting the ball. After surveying the defensive line, the quarterback took the snap, pivoted left, and handed the ball to Mack, who then bulldozed his way through a wall of defenders and was now bearing down on Sikes.

The linebacker had already been pummeled by the big guy once in the game, when he lined up in the fullback position to deliver a wham block to Mack, who doubled as a defensive tackle, in order to let Gilmer's tailback scamper by on a trap play. Instead, Mack plowed into Sikes at the line of scrimmage and crumpled him on contact.

With the incident still fresh in Sikes's memory, the junior adapted his approach and plunged into Mack's legs instead of hitting him high up, throwing him off his balance, so the other Buckeye defensive players could tackle him to the ground, just shy of a first down.

The refs gave their verdict: "Short by an inch! Turnover on downs! Gilmer football!"

The crowd erupted—and now Gilmer had the ball on their 18-yard line with 1:10 left on the clock. The showdown between Gilmer and Gladewater harkened back to another power match three decades earlier that had become the stuff of East Texas lore: the 1984 Gladewater-Daingerfield playoff game.

The two schools entered the contest each boasting a 13-0 record. The winner would advance to the semifinals of the state playoffs.

Daingerfield had won the previous season's 3A state title, and had ended the season with 631 points, allowing only eight points to rivals that season, and zero on defense. (They still hold the NFHS national record for the most shutouts in a single season.)

The contest ended in a 27-27 tie after Daingerfield blocked Gladewater's extra point attempt with 17 seconds left. At the time, the University Interscholastic League (UIL) hadn't implemented overtime, so the team that advanced would be the one who had more penetrations.

Daingerfield had six, Gladewater had five. Daingerfield advanced.

"I was a junior in high school, sitting in the end zone at Tyler's Rose Stadium, watching the greatest game I had ever seen," recalled the Buckeyes' coach, Jeff Traylor, a Gilmer kid. "I wanted to be in that moment so bad. It's why I wanted to become a coach."

In East Texas, coaches are at the pinnacle of their town because a community's identity *is* its high school football team. The 1984 teams were led by Daingerfield's Dennis Alexander and Gladewater's Jack Murphy— both legendary head coaches. Each would leave his imprint on a future generation of East Texas high school football coaches, including Traylor.

"The matchup was what you'd dream about," said Traylor. "Rose was the premier place in those days. It was Cowboys Stadium in my eyes."

***

Three decades later, many in the crowd had that iconic game on their minds when Gilmer faced Gladewater in Longview's Lobo stadium, the Rose Stadium of its day and a prime location for a playoff game. Lobo had Division-1 amenities, including a press box and massive stands that could hold the Lobo Band's Big Green Marching Machine. Those lucky enough to be in the stadium had waited in line for hours to claim their seats. Beyond the Jumbotron, an overflow crowd from the stadium sat on blankets in a grassy bowl to watch the game. The only hindrance to their view of the field was a rectangular bed of bushes that spelled out "Lobos," just in case they forgot whose house they were in.

The Gilmer-Gladewater matchup had kicked off with each team's superstars demonstrating their value on the region's biggest stage. Gilmer received the ball first, and immediately showed why it had one of the most prolific offenses in Texas high school football history. Quarterback McLane Carter took a short snap on Gilmer's 10-yard line and tossed a short swing pass to running back Kris Boyd. The play was designed to give the Buckeyes some breathing room by attacking the outside, since the ever-dangerous Mack was known for clogging the middle. Boyd took the simple toss and surprised Gladewater's defenders by turning on the jets and going 90 yards for an opening drive touchdown.

Just like that it was 7-0 Gilmer.

This was completely counter to Gladewater's game plan. While Gilmer was known for its stratospheric scoring and flashy, high-tempo offense, the Bears were a grind-it-out team that was going to run the ball, eat up the clock, and stand its ground on defense.

Gladewater Coach John Berry stuck with the winning plan that had taken his team this far. When the Bears' next drive wasn't fruitful and Gilmer got the ball back, Berry's best player, Daylon Mack, delivered a hit on quarterback McLane Carter that made the entire stadium gasp. It let everyone know that the Bears weren't going anywhere, and it allowed Gladewater to recapture momentum. On its next drive, they scored by way of a 15-yard quarterback keeper.

After a failed two-point conversion, the score was 7-6.

Gilmer responded with an attack on the Bears with the vertical passing game. Senior quarterback McLane Carter had a 74 percent completion percentage on the year. His receivers didn't help his numbers this time though; and after consecutive dropped passes, Gilmer was forced to punt.

Gladewater took over on its own 48-yard line, and decisively marched down the field on the backs of its power running game. The drive was finished off by Mack taking it in from 11 yards out. After the two-point conversion was good, the score now read Gladewater 14, Gilmer 7.

"Daylon was so powerful," Gilmer defensive coordinator Todd Barr later recalled. "He was the perfect back. If he's on your team, he's going to get you four or five yards per down."

While Mack's night had already been impressive, it was the next drive that cemented his status as one of the top high school players in Texas.

After Gladewater intercepted a pass from Gilmer utility player Blake Lynch, the Bears started on its own 34 with the crowd on their side. The first play was a handoff to Mack on a fullback dive. He took it 10 yards before five different defenders eventually took him to the ground. The crowd loved it. He was a man among boys.

Berry called Mack's number three more times on this drive before he crossed the goal line for his second touchdown of the night. Gladewater was now up 21-7, and in complete control of the game.

Gilmer had not been tested since it played at Tatum during the third week of the season and squeaked out a narrow victory. But the program prided itself on its culture of toughness, hard work, and resilience.

"We focus on outworking other teams," said Kurt Traylor. "You look at the top five programs every year. It's the same ones.

Our kids believed they were going to be successful. They truly believed they outworked everyone. The work we put in the dark will shine in the light. I hate to say the word brainwash, but we believed it at Gilmer."

The staff also shared these sentiments, relentlessly out-preparing other coaches.

"When I joined the staff, I was in awe," said Kerry Lane, a young, promising coach on Traylor's staff. "I had never seen that many good coaches on one staff before. Gilmer is on a whole different level than any other place in this area, a level that would rival most college programs. You've got 30-minute position meetings every day, on both sides of the ball. Coaches fine combed every second of practice to make sure they're at peak efficiency. It works though. Our kids didn't flinch in a game, but you saw other teams crumble."

Gilmer responded to its two-touchdown deficit by adjusting its planned attack on the Bears. Rather than rely on the vertical passing game, the players started doing a zone-read play called "Thelma," where Carter would hand the ball off to Boyd from the shotgun. They ran the same play five straight times averaging almost eight yards a play. The end result was another Kris Boyd touchdown.

Deciding to gamble after reclaiming the momentum, Gilmer did an onside kick and got the ball back. Eight plays later, Boyd found the end zone again. The score now read 21-21 as the first half came to a close. The atmosphere was electric. People knew this was going to go down to the wire.

***

In 2014, Coach John Berry was in his first season as a head coach at Gladewater. After serving as an assistant under John King at perennial powerhouse Longview High School, he joined Gladewater in 2010 when his friend Jerrod Baugh got the job. After three years of turning around a flailing Gladewater program, Baugh took the Bears to the playoffs and won three games before the team fell to Argyle in the regional semifinals.

The 2014 season's expectations were high, especially with Mack being a senior. And then, adversity hit. Baugh had to resign from the head coaching position for personal reasons, and Berry was thrust into his first head job with a group widely regarded as Gladewater's most talented team since the famed 1984 squad.

In contrast, the seasoned Jeff Traylor was in year 15 of his tenure at Gilmer, which had competed in four state titles and won two. With a steady staff and well-defined culture, Traylor was a fixture in the minds of Gilmer boys, who dreamed about playing for the Buckeye Varsity football team at an early age; he'd created a pipeline of talent from elementary school to the gridiron.

"What makes Gilmer so different from other places in Texas is the expectation our community and our coaches have for our kids," said Gilmer principal Brian Bowman. "What I mean by that is our kids, well before they get into 7th grade, know what is expected of them. They said *yes sir* and *no sir, yes ma'am* and *no ma'am* to every teacher; they knew they'd have mandatory tutorials before they went to football practice once or twice a week and that they were going to lift weights."

"My oldest son won a state championship his freshman year, and my middle son was on the 2014 team. I remember talking to my youngest son who was in third grade at the time, and he said to me, 'Dad, am I going to get a state championship ring when I'm in high school?' And I said, 'Yeah, you probably will—if you stay in the Gilmer program.'"

***

The second half started dully after the scoring surge that highlighted the end of the first. Both teams were aggressive, but, ultimately, both were forced to punt. Then the field action slowly turned into a heavyweight prize fight with both sides trading shots. Gladewater led first this time using Mack as a decoy on a counter run. The run garnered 25 yards and a touchdown. Gladewater 28, Gilmer 21.

Gilmer answered by letting a transfer player, Blake Lynch, show off his all-world athleticism. Lynch frustrated every defense he faced because of his versatility. He could line up at quarterback, running back, or even wide receiver. On this drive, highlighted by his direct snap draw from the quarterback position, he took it 20 yards for a touchdown. The attempted two-point conversion failed, and the Buckeyes trailed 28-27.

Again, Gilmer tried an onside kick, but a costly penalty kept them from executing. On the game's tenth series for both sides, Mack reemerged to convert two fourth down runs for Gladewater along with another touchdown, his fourth of the game. Gladewater was now up 35-27 in the fourth quarter. It was a gut punch to the Buckeyes.

"Unbelievable," Kurt Traylor later recalled. "Maybe the best high school player we've ever played against."

To add insult to injury, the ensuing kick return resulted in a penalty for blocking in the back, and now the Buckeyes would start on their own six-yard line.

Gilmer needed a big play.

McLane Carter delivered. First, he hit Nick Smith on a 44-yard pass that got the ball at midfield and followed that up by connecting with Quinn Fluellen for 20 yards. A couple of plays later, Kris Boyd ran it in for the touchdown from 10 yards out.

The Buckeyes again attempted the two-point conversion but failed to bring the game to a tie. The score was 35-33 with Gladewater in the lead late in the fourth quarter. Gilmer would gamble one more time. The onside kick failed; Gladewater got it.

The Bears were starting on the Gilmer 48-yard line, and penalties hurt any progress they'd initially made. Then, in a pivotal moment, Gladewater's running back took the handoff, found a crease, and ran to daylight. The rush of energy from inside the stadium seemed to confirm that this was indeed going to be the nail in the coffin for the Buckeyes. But then at the last moment, the running back decided to go to the ground at the 27-yard line. The motive was to stay in bounds and run out the clock, since there was no way Gilmer could stop Mack. Berry ordered his staff to do what had worked all game, give the ball to Mack. The first play was a dive call that earned six yards. The second play, however, only yielded one yard.

That Mack was getting tired became clear to the defense and Gilmer coaching staff.

At third and three, Berry called for the quarterback keeper, an unexpected change for the defense. It only worked for one yard. It would be fourth and two.

While Gilmer's defense was preparing for its most important play of the game, the rest of the players on the Buckeyes' sideline were on their hands and knees drawing an imaginary line in front of them to offer inspiration to the guys on the field.

During a University of Alabama game the week before, Navy SEAL Marcus Luttrell had done the pregame talk about how he'd achieved the impossible. Lying with a broken back after a battle with the Taliban, Luttrell was the lone survivor and was badly wounded. To move himself, he would pull his gun out, draw a line with it, and then pull himself to the line—a process he repeated over and over again for several hundred yards, crawling to safety and escaping capture.

Coach Traylor told his players about Luttrell's story and showed a video of his talk to the Buckeyes on a day leading up to the game.

Recalls Alan Metzel, an assistant coach and pastor in Gilmer, "Traylor told the players that there's going to be a tough time in the game when our backs are against the wall and we're going to have to draw a line in the sand to take down Daylon Mack."

As soon as Jackson Sikes and the Gilmer defense stopped Mack short, Metzel and fellow offensive play caller, Matt Turner, went to work giving their players signals for their next moves.

With the ball on their own 18-yard line, the first play was a 12-yard pass from Carter to Lynch who immediately got out of bounds. They then took a shot down field. Incomplete.

Another incomplete pass followed—this one to the right.

Things started looking dismal for the Buckeyes. It was third down, they had no more timeouts, and the clock was dwindling. Metzel suggested they run a hitch-and-pitch, a downfield pass to a receiver who then pitches it off to another offensive player upon making the catch. This particular pass would go to wide receiver Nick Smith, who would then flip it to tailback Kris Boyd.

Jeff Traylor cautioned everyone about how physical the Bears' defensive back was going to be on Smith. "He's pressing him! He's pressing him!"

Metzel chimed in, "It's fine. He'll push him up. He'll swat him by. *This* is why we work it."

So, on the snap, Smith fired off the ball and started driving his man back. But Gladewater's defensive back was locked in on Smith, who answered by taking him back one more yard than he's supposed to. He then put his hand on the DB's hip, swatted him by, and pushed back looking for the ball from McLane Carter.

As usual, Carter delivered a strike.

At the same time, Boyd streaked by just as Smith was being tackled. Smith pitched the ball to Boyd, who caught it, and then took over all the way to the Gladewater 45-yard line.

"If there ever was a play that illustrated why we make practice so hard, and we prepared so much, then that play was it to me," said Lane, describing the play years later. "That was the best look at what our kids were. They repped it, they were confident, and they executed it in the biggest moment of the game."

An incomplete pass from Carter followed, but McLane quickly redeemed that play with a completed pass to another Gilmer receiver on the 23-yard line after scrambling to the right.

With under one minute to play and no timeouts, the Buckeyes shocked the Gladewater defense—who were expecting a pass—and called a draw play for Kris Boyd, who had lined up at running back. He dashed through the open seam and dove into the end zone for the go-ahead touchdown. After adding a two-point conversion, Gilmer took the lead with the score of 41-35.

"That's what's special," Metzel said. "That play was called on the previous Sunday. It wasn't luck. Jeff always says, 'Think people, not plays.' You put it in the hands of a guy that can go, and Kris did it. Everyone went nuts. That was an amazing feeling right there."

Gladewater got the ball back for one final last second play, and it failed.

The final score on the Jumbotron: Gilmer 41, Gladewater 35. The atmosphere was electric.

While the kids were celebrating in the locker room, eating their post-game snickers and chocolate milk, Traylor looked at his team and foresaw the future.

"We're about to win this whole thing," he said.

Jeff Traylor embraces his daughter, Jaci, after Gilmer defeats Gladewater in what many locals deem the greatest football game ever played in East Texas. (Courtesy of Ruel Felipe)

Student workers hold up the Gilmer Buckeye sign for the football team to bust through as the players make their way to the sidelines on Friday nights. (Courtesy of Ruel Felipe)

"In East Texas, football drives the town."
--Kurt Traylor

Chapter 2: Birthplace of the Yamboree

In Texas, high school football culture is synonymous with small town culture. On fall Fridays, townspeople flock to the seats of high school stadiums across the state, all waiting with anticipation to see *their* team play.

The buildup to kickoff begins hours before the fans arrive. The afternoon of the game, the circadian rhythms of small towns shift to "Football Standard Time." Classes let out early for pep rallies, and the entire school—in home team swag—spills into the yellow fluorescence of the gym to the beat of the marching band. In matching pompoms and hair ribbons, cheerleaders introduce the football team to the crowd, which roars as players wave to the elementary-aged classes in attendance all dreaming about the day when they'll be old enough to represent their school under the bright lights.

Thoroughly inebriated with school spirit, the crowd is now prepped for the big game. Even beyond the campus, the town is abuzz, and local businesses close down early to dash to the stadium and nab the best seats. Even the mothers of the players have their own ritual, gathering together with volunteers to make home-made food packages for their boys and their coaches.

"No college or professional game can match the intensity of high school playing fields," observed Geoff Winningham in his elegiac essay "Friday Night Heroes," published in *Texas Monthly*. "A winning football team is as much a symbol of vitality as rising bank deposits or a new Dairy Queen. It reaffirms everyone's faith in the community."

Small town football was birthed in rural Texas and continues to live on across the state and beyond, although 85 percent of Texans now live in big cities. It's a testament to the power of football culture that towns like Gilmer (population: 5,000) write the blueprint for Friday night fall games in El Paso, Dallas-Fort Worth, San Antonio, Austin, and Houston.

High school football may be the purest expression of the game, a belief as much as a sport. In high school stadiums, football is still uncommercialized by universities and pro leagues. Alumni donations, that rise and fall on the team's success in NCAA football, don't matter in high school sports, and the billion-dollar machine that calls itself the "NFL" has left varsity football unmarred.

"In these one-school towns, *everybody* lives through their teams," said Gilmer High School defensive coach Wayne Coleman. "The sad thing is you leave and go somewhere else and you're thinking it should always be like this, which it's not. You don't realize until later just how great an atmosphere it is."

Coleman experienced this firsthand, coaching at Marshall and Jacksonville high schools before leaving the football-obsessed area to serve as a head coach in other parts of the state. He then got to experience East Texas football again, this time with his old friend, Jeff Traylor, at Gilmer.

***

Gilmer is a landlocked patch of East Texas named in honor of U.S. Secretary of the Navy, Thomas Walker Gilmer. He, along with Abel Parker Upshur, a former Justice of the Virginia

Supreme Court, pushed to have Texas annexed to the Union in the 1840s. After annexation succeeded in 1845, the Texas Legislature immortalized them by naming a rural northwest county "Upshur" and its county seat "Gilmer."

The more time passes, the more Gilmer seems to remain the same.

"For the past 50 years, the town has been largely unchanged," said long-time resident, Pete Herrmann.

"We have a local trucking company in town, and we have an electrical company in town, Robroy, that employs several people," he said. "Our steel plant closed and then reopened. At one time, it employed 5,000 and now it's like 1,000. Dairy farming has almost disappeared, but forestry and timber are still going."

Gilmer's greatest source of pride—in addition to football and the Buckeyes—is the annual East Texas Yamboree Festival, a four-day celebration of the region's mainstay crop, held every October. Founded in 1935, and held every year since, with a hiatus during World War II, the Yamboree—which is vital for the town's economy—attracts about 100,000 visitors, who stream into town for the festival's pie contests, cattle judging, and a carnival held right on the courthouse square.

"It's a homecoming more than anything," said Pete Herrmann. "It's something for people from here to come back and see people they normally don't get to see all of the time."

One of the festival highlights is the coronation of the Yamboree Queen. Eligible participants sell tickets to the festival, and the one who sells the most is crowned.

"People will say that when a granddaughter is born, the grandparents start putting money away so the grandbaby can be queen when she's older," said Herrmann.

While Gilmer has taken great pride in the festival, the town's history isn't without its blemishes. Social progress didn't move fast in this part of the state. In the 1970's at the courthouse just off the square, there was still a "White's Only" sign that hung. Mind you, the Civil Rights Act was passed in 1964 outlawing things like this.

There were periods of time where race and social class both divided the community. Everyone knew who the free-lunch kids were, who lived in a single-parent family, and who had money. Wealthy mansions of attorneys and owners of East Texas lumber mills were only a few miles away from communities like Vinegar Hill, an all-Black neighborhood that was ridden with poverty.

"We had a lot of problems – drugs, race issues, things like that," said Class of '95 Gilmer graduate and current Buckeye coach, Keith Tate. "A lot of people thought Gilmer was a place that had a lot of potential when I was growing up. It just never achieved anything that was long lasting."

* * *

Church, family, and football formed the blueprint of Gilmer culture, and no one embodied those values more than Billy and Linda Traylor, who raised three boys—Jeff, Kurt, and Andy—two of whom would change Gilmer football history. In fact, the Traylors lived across the street from the football stadium, where all three boys would play when they were in high school, and where Kurt and Jeff would turn the Buckeyes into a championship team.

"Jeff was always in love with sports," Linda recalled. "When he was a young kid, he watched Dallas Cowboys games with his grandfather every Sunday and he could quote every statistic about each player."

The Traylors were pillars of the community who instilled discipline and a work ethic in their children; the boys' fierce competitiveness came naturally.

"From girlfriends to eating, Jeff and I always competed," said Kurt. "What is amazing, though, is that we never competed on who made the best grades, even though my parents drilled the importance of education into us, especially because they were both educators and Dad had been a principal in another district before he decided to take a job as an administrator in Gilmer."

Growing up, the brothers had their eyes on football glory, but, in fact, it was girls basketball and not football that was known for its success when Kurt and Jeff were at Gilmer High.

"If you were a Lady Buckeye, you could get a free meal at the Dairy Queen," said Stacy Crews, a Gilmer graduate and current Girls Coordinator for the Buckeyes.

Even though the football team was never consistently good, they did have some stellar moments. In 1981, they went to state but were beaten by Cameron Yoe. In 1985, they went three rounds deep and repeated that in 1990 and 1991.

"That's about it. In the 70s they were horrible. I think back in the day they were pretty good, like in the 50s and 60s," said Kurt. "I don't want to say the team was in disarray when we played, but we didn't have a lot of pride. You could go to a game and there might be 100 people in the stands. The kids weren't excited to play football when they got to high school."

Both brothers longed to play under winning coaches in neighboring towns, like Dennis Alexander from Daingerfield and Jack Murphy from Gladewater.

"The White Oak coaches—Andy Griffin and Dan Noll—I had so much respect for those guys," said Jeff. "I wanted us to be more like that. I played for three different coaches when I was coming up in school. I wanted Gilmer to be steady."

After helping lead the '85 Gilmer team to a 10-3 record with a share of the district championship, Traylor elected to attend Stephen F. Austin State University (SFA) in Nacogdoches, following in the footsteps of his parents, and walk on to the football team.

"I was an undisciplined kid who didn't come from a very good program," said Jeff. "I was basically a big fish in a small pond at Gilmer. I thought I was better than I was."

SFA, on the other hand, was coming off a Gulf South Conference Championship season. They were talented, and their leader, Jim Hess, was highly respected.

"He was great," added Jeff. "He could make everyone feel like the most important person in the room."

"I was just a walk-on practice player. I played tight end, wound up playing two years and never touched the field. I hurt my shoulder my second year, realized I wasn't very good, and then hung it up—but I *did* go on to win a couple intramural basketball championships after that," he said.

The consummate competitor, Jeff was even known to keep his own statistics in intramurals.

One of his teammates on those intramural teams was future White Oak head basketball coach Ron Boyett, who, like Jeff, would one day become an East Texas legend.

After Jeff quit playing football, he still had a clear vision of who he wanted to be and where he wanted to go. And he was trying to get there as fast as possible.

"I always knew I wanted to be a coach. I majored in kinesiology. I always wanted to be the head coach at Gilmer," he said. "I still remember one time when Kurt and I were coaching together at another school, and we'd go scout a team that was playing at Gilmer. And Gilmer would be playing their butt off and then, all of a sudden, they'd lay down in the second half or do something stupid and get beat."

During these bleak moments, Jeff saw a kernel of hope. Although Kurt was skeptical, Jeff knew that the team had a future.

"I wasn't convinced," Kurt said. "I was like 'alright, bro.' But Jeff believed in what it could be."

Desmond Pollard (#8) was loved by the entire Gilmer community, and the Buckeyes chose to honor their fallen teammate by dedicating the 2014 season to him. (Courtesy of Ruel Felipe)

"The community eventually came together in such an incredible way. He was one of Gilmer's own."
--Matt Turner

Chapter 3: The Ultimate Slogan

Jeff Traylor wanted championship teams, and to get them he instituted an intensive week-long boot camp designed to physically and mentally test the new crop of students who wanted to play football: the Buckeye Maker.

The Buckeye Maker was a tradition that Jeff brought to Gilmer after working under Coach Danny Long at Jacksonville. It tested the mettle of players and prospects with mat drills, field contests, and other conditioning activities designed to bring the overweight, sedentary, and otherwise out-of-shape to their knees and then rebuild them. For kids on the fence about playing varsity football the upcoming season, the Buckeye Maker was an early test of will and grit that separated the true believers from the half-hearted. It was so hard that it was known by a different name in its early days.

"It used to be called the Nutcracker," said Kerry Lane, a young and promising coach on Jeff Traylor's staff, "but people got mad about that."

According to Alan Metzel, an assistant coach who also served as one of the community's pastors, "It was critical to establishing accountability because each player had to perform at his peak at every second of the game."

If you did well, the coaches rewarded you in front of your peers, and if didn't do well in a session, you were called out and given some tough love.

"We told them that we were going to hold them to the highest standard. And we did that because we loved them and wanted them to succeed," Metzel said.

In February 2014, the team officially began its quest for a championship season with the start of boot camp. The 2013 team had finished 11-2 and gone three rounds into the playoffs, but had failed to capture a district championship, a feat they had missed only three times in the last 15 years. The 2014 Buckeyes were hungry and focused.

And they also had their quarterback, McLane Carter, back with the team.

***

McLane Carter was born in Mesquite, Texas, in the Dallas area, and the family lived there until he went to kindergarten, before moving him to Canton, where he started elementary school. Canton, a small country town in East Texas, was a far cry from Dallas. It's main claim to fame was its gigantic outdoor flea market.

The family moved to Canton, in part, to reunite McLane and his mother with her son, G.J., whom she'd had with her former husband, Gary Joe Kinne. A new coach at Canton High School, Kinne had incurred some wrath among football parents by using G.J. on the field more than the other players. But nepotism wasn't the driving factor; sheer talent was.

G.J. was known statewide as one of the most promising high school players in Texas. He was a phenom who would go on to play Division I football at Tulsa and then play for five seasons in the NFL.

Approaching his junior year in high school—when his younger brother, McLane, was still in grade school—G.J. was riding high and had helped the football team win 16 games in a two-year period, the most in the school's history. Then, the unthinkable happened. In April of 2005, a rift between Kinne and a player's father led to bloodshed. The father, Jeffrey Doyle Robertson, had marched into Canton High School's coaches' office with an automatic handgun and fired a bullet into Coach Gary Joe Kinne's chest.

Kinne was rushed to the hospital, where he underwent multiple surgeries to repair his damaged liver and remove the bullet. Robertson was arrested with aggravated assault with a deadly weapon and sentenced to prison.

In the aftermath of the shooting, Kinne spent the offseason rehabbing his body to return to the sidelines to coach his son. He came back just in time for the 2005 season where he led Canton to a 12-win season, and G.J. was named 3A Player of the Year. The Canton community, however, remained divided on the entire incident and Gary Joe left the school at the end of the season to take an assistant coaching post at Baylor University. Mrs. Carter decided that a new change of scenery would be good for her two boys too, even with it being G.J.'s senior year.

The choice of town was no accident. The family was impressed with Gilmer's football program and Jeff Traylor's ability to develop quarterbacks, and their decision to move to Gilmer caused quite the dustup. A big reason was because Canton had beaten Gilmer in the 2005 state playoffs, largely because of G.J.'s quarterback play. When news of the transfer became official, it spread like wildfire throughout East Texas.

Coaches began complaining to the University Interscholastic League (UIL), the oversight body for high school football in Texas, about Jeff Traylor "recruiting" Kinne, which was forbidden by league rules.

"It was an iffy moment because Jeff was giving a fresh start to G.J., a kid who had just suffered a terrible trauma and needed a football home," said Kurt. "He'd known the family and was trying to help him."

After some discussion, the matter was settled when the UIL signed off on the move. The air never completely cleared, but G.J. joined the Buckeyes and played for them during his senior year.

For McLane, the move to Gilmer was sum positive.

"I remember writing on my paper *March 28, 2006,* on my first day in third grade at Gilmer," recalled Carter. "It was a huge change, for the better. The school had so much more diversity compared to Canton, and I remember being struck by the number of African American students in my class. It was a great thing for me."

Gilmer welcomed the Carter family warmly, and McLane met a friend who would become an indelible figure in his life, Desmond Pollard, who'd also moved to Gilmer in the third grade. McLane thrived in Gilmer. He eventually played quarterback on his grade level team and loved it—but he was small and not an obvious pick for the Buckeyes Varsity team.

His chances grew slimmer when in 2012 the UIL had announced its realignment for the next two years and created a district that included Gilmer as well as recent state champions Henderson and Tyler-Chapel Hill. Newspapers dubbed it the "District of Doom" because of the overwhelming amount of talent. The realigned district placed the Buckeyes with other great teams, but it didn't bode well for smaller players, like Carter.

"My best friend, Desmond Pollard and guys like Kris Boyd and Chase Tate, these guys were already making big plays for the varsity football team as sophomores," said Carter. "Kris was getting offers from like TCU. He was a freak. But I was still very small. I just wasn't ready to compete in that region. We were playing Henderson and Kilgore. There were a lot of grown men we were going against."

Questioning whether or not he would get to play quarterback at Gilmer, Carter decided after his sophomore year to move south to Salado to live with his father and play for Salado High School.

"They (Salado) weren't a very talented team, but I had started to grow," he said.

"Grow" was an understatement. In the offseason between his sophomore and junior years, he'd morphed into a serious contender, going from 5'9, 140 lbs. to 6'2, 180 lbs.

"We didn't go to the playoffs, but individually I had a pretty dominant season. I always threw for 300-400 yards," he said.

But even with the individual success, McLane wanted to rejoin his Buckeye teammates. Once his junior season was over, he officially returned to Gilmer, this time more motivated.

"When McLane came back to Gilmer, he had matured a lot," said Coach Alan Metzel. "He had a different sense of appreciation for the team. His work ethic was improved. He wanted to be better, and he didn't want to be satisfied."

Taking his focus a step further, Carter made the decision to live in a duplex less than one mile away from the fieldhouse, and rather him go from house to house, his parents decided to let McLane stay in the same place the entire time. His mom and dad would just rotate who stayed with him.

McLane had returned not only for football but also for his mother and his friends in Gilmer, the place he called home. He'd especially missed the good friend he'd met in third grade, Desmond Pollard.

***

Pollard and his family had lived in the Los Angeles area before coming to Gilmer in third grade, so he and McLane bonded over their new adjustment to country life.

"At the time we lived out in the middle of nowhere - hundreds of acres of land. We had three ponds stocked with bass. We could play in the woods and stuff. I remember we'd go over to our friends, Brady and John English's house, and we'd ride our bikes across the field to get there. The English family showed pigs, so they had a pig farm. We were in awe of that," Carter said, looking back on his boyhood friendship.

"We were both in a place that was new, so that might've been why we clung to each other so much. In the summer, especially, Desmond started staying with us for longer periods of time. At first it was like three days, then it was five days, then two weeks, and, sometimes, even longer."

Desmond's long stays helped his struggling mother, and he came to see the Carters as his family.

"Sometimes he'd cry when we took him home. His mom was doing the best she could, but he was just in a rough neighborhood. His brothers were older, so they weren't ever home."

Carter's parents loved Desmond, too. When the family decided to move to another home in Gilmer, it made sure to designate one of the rooms to be Desmond's.

"He was my brother. My older brother, G.J., he was his little brother. He had friends. He loved his mom, and he saw his mom. But he became a part of our family too," said Carter.

The friendship thrived and continued into their adult years. Then, tragedy struck.

On March 2, 2014, McLane, G.J., and Desmond were in Mesquite visiting an old family friend of G.J.'s. It was the start of Gilmer's spring break. McLane and Desmond were late in their junior years at Gilmer, and G.J. was already playing in the NFL as a quarterback. The Buckeyes had completed boot camp earlier in February, but Desmond was restricted from participating because a local doctor noticed some irregularity in his blood. Pollard's family had a history of less-than-ideal health, and the coaching staff wanted to make sure they played it safe in the offseason.

"He was extremely down about it," said Carter. "His blood pressure had been pretty high, and the coaches just wanted him to chill out."

While hanging out at their friend Houston's house, the boys decided to play a pickup game of basketball in a local private school's vacant gym. It was cold outside, and they were bored.

"We told Desmond to kind of chill or whatever, but it's hard to tell a senior in high school that you can't play in a pickup basketball game," said Carter. "Desmond was a hooper, too. People could throw him alley-oops, and he'd do some crazy dunks. You have to remember, Desmond was now 6'3, 200 pounds."

The guys rounded up enough local players to have a 3-on-3 game.

"There were no cell phones ringing. We were just having a good time. Just brotherhood," said Carter.

About 30 minutes into the game, Houston and Desmond were on a fast break play that led to Houston tossing an alley-oop up to Desmond, who was being guarded by G.J. Demonstrating his incredible athleticism, Pollard leaped up, grabbed the ball, and jammed it on him. All of the remaining players yelled with enthusiasm at what they just saw. It was just another example of Desmond's extraordinary athleticism.

But as each player started to run down to the other end of the floor to keep up with the pace of the game, Desmond wasn't running with them.

"We all turned our back and started running back down the floor," said Carter. "I was on the left-hand side. Then there was this big thud, like a brick hitting the ground. And there he was—eyes rolling, foaming at the mouth, shaking real hard."

"I remember running up to him. We kind of thought he was joking. Someone said, 'Man, stop playing!' They thought he was joking. Then more foam came out of his mouth and his chest, and we knew it wasn't a game."

Houston screamed to the others to call 911, while G.J.'s girlfriend, Summer, began giving Desmond mouth-to-mouth resuscitation. McLane ran outside seeking out anyone who was available.

"I sprinted outside, and it was so cold. I looked for people, but no one was out there. I just remember running back in and seeing my brother with his hands on his head saying, 'I knew I shouldn't have let him play.'"

Finally, the ambulance arrived at the gym, and the paramedics put Pollard on a stretcher and loaded him into the ambulance. Because no one was allowed to travel with him, the friends hurried to the emergency room, where they gathered in the waiting room until a doctor appeared 45 minutes later to deliver an update.

Desmond had died from heart failure. There was nothing they could have done.

"I started picking up chairs in the waiting room and screaming-crying," said Carter. "It was a different kind of crying from everybody else."

McLane's mother and father raced up the icy roads of I-20 to comfort their sons and grieve over the other son they'd lost.

"I remember my dad coming in—and he's a tough dude. I don't think I ever saw him shed a tear in his life. And I just saw him break down the moment he arrived," said McLane.

"I'll never forget I got a phone call from G.J.," said Matt Turner. "You could just tell from the moment you heard his voice that he was distraught. He'd just seen his brother die."

The boys had to make other phone calls to family, teammates, and coaches. Sometimes, McLane had to surrender those duties to his big brother because it was so painful.

"It was just hard making those calls when you are not even a senior in high school," said Carter. "You need a grown up to be making those kinds of calls. I was just so tired. I could barely move."

What began as a family grieving extended to an entire team.

"It was such a shock when we found out," said Todd Barr, long-time defensive coordinator for Jeff Traylor. "Our team was devastated. He was a kid who had so much potential. Everyone loved him. We just tumbled and had to collectively refocus."

"The community eventually came together in such an incredible way," said Turner. "He was one of Gilmer's own. It caused us all to reflect, find strength in each other, and that's what we did."

Jeff Traylor traditionally had let the seniors select a slogan for the upcoming season. This year's choice was obvious. The 2014 slogan was going to be #DEZign8 in honor of Desmond's team number.

"I have never met a group of men handle a situation so well," said McLane. "Our coaches were sympathetic and understanding but also very positive. When this situation hit, the drive that staff had for the success of our class just kind of shot through the roof. They weren't going to let us fail."

"The slogan that the team created—#DEZign8—we went back to it when the days were long and tired. It totally re-focused everyone on the team," said Metzel. "We were able to kick into another level of execution."

***

One of those crucial figures during the crisis was the Buckeyes' quarterback coach, Alan Metzel.

"Coach Metzel was the best man in my life," Carter said. "I cannot say enough about him."

"He's one notch lower than Jesus Christ," said Kurt Traylor.

Originally from Oak Ridge, Tennessee, Metzel moved to the East Texas area in middle school when his stepfather, a minister, was assigned to preach at a country church in Gilmer.

"My biological dad left when I was two when my mom was pregnant with my brother," said Metzel. "A year or so later my stepfather, George Metzel, came into East Tennessee. He had been a hellion, played music with Chuck Berry and Jerry Lee Lewis. He had lived a pretty rough life."

"Then he started dating my mom and came to know the Lord. It was an absolute transformation. Then he decided to go into the ministry. My mom is a powerful lady. She's affected a lot of people."

Alan graduated from Harmony High School, another school system in Upshur County, and then attended college in Florida. Upon graduation, his old coach from high school, Jed Whitaker, gave him a call. He had taken on the role of head football coach and invited Alan to join his staff. Metzel jumped at the chance.

After valuable tenures at both Harmony and Union Grove High School, Jeff Traylor came calling. Metzel joined Gilmer's staff in 2001. His stepfather had started pastoring a church in the same area just one year earlier.

Six years later, George Metzel passed away, and the small country church he established needed a leader. Alan answered the call. He's been serving both institutions ever since.

"Alan is like this rock that anybody that has a problem can go to," said Wayne Coleman, a coach who had mentored Jeff when they were coaches at Jacksonville. "He's the guy that you want to do your daughter's wedding and your parent's funeral."

Over the years, Metzel has especially developed a reputation for his inspirational text messages and letters that he sends out to people of all ages and walks of life.

"I have an older son who is coaching at ETBU [East Texas Baptist University]," said Brian Bowman, the principal of Gilmer High School. "And I also have a son who works with TCU [Texas Christian University]. Every single day since they graduated, Alan Metzel sends them an uplifting quote and Bible verse by text. He does that to so many people it's crazy. He's probably the most pure, godly, Christ-centered individual that I've ever worked with."

"If it was your birthday or any other important day, you were going to get a card," said Kurt Traylor. "Now, is he firey and competitive? Lord yes! He loves to compete and win."

Metzel provided the team with great comfort after the loss of Pollard, but he also was the perfect combination of both counselor and competitor for a quarterback who had always been labeled "the little brother" or "the late bloomer." And now, they were solely focused on honoring their fallen teammate.

"I had a vision of what I wanted this year to be like. We all did," Carter said.

Members of the Marshall Mavericks coaching staff pose for a picture inside the Houston Astrodome after winning the 1990 5A state championship. Danny Long, Matt Turner, and Wayne Coleman all learned under Marshall's legendary head coach, Dennis Parker, during this time. (Courtesy of Wayne Coleman)

"Dennis Parker is like the Dallas Cowboys, and I love the Dallas Cowboys."
--Danny Long

Chapter 4: The Marshall Legacy

Dr. Carl Sagan once stated, "You have to know the past to understand the present."

That's certainly true with understanding East Texas high school football, where knowledge has been passed down from coach to coach and program to program.

The Gilmer coaching tree has become one of the most trusted pedigrees in the East Texas region today. Several other coaching staffs have been birthed out of working with the Buckeyes, and many of them are head coaches. But Gilmer is also part of a much larger tree, one that stretches hundreds of miles south, just outside of San Antonio.

Coach Frank Arnold
Frank Arnold's coaching career lasted 20 years. After coaching stops in San Antonio ISD's Sam Houston, Jefferson, Holmes, and MacArthur High Schools, Coach Arnold signed on to work for what would be his last school, Converse Judson. Jerry Sanders was the head coach at the time, and the Judson Rockets were in the middle of a program renovation. After going 9-40-1 during the five years before Arnold joined, the Rockets steadily improved going 30-4 over the next three years, winning district championships every year along the way.

In 1979, Coach Sanders officially retired and turned the program over to Arnold. The next four years were wildly successful under his mentee's direction. The Rockets went 42-9 over four years and captured the 1983 5A state championship. Arnold was viewed as a community pillar, adored by his players and their families. In return, Arnold also recognized how talented his staff was on both sides of the ball. Both of his coordinators were in high demand for other head jobs. On offense, he had Dennis Parker, a former offensive lineman from Oklahoma who had joined his staff from the college level. On defense, he had D.W. Rutledge, a native Texan who had played for and coached under in-state legend Jim Wacker when he won a national championship at Texas Lutheran. Both were incredible motivators and organizers.

Only months after winning the state title in 1983, Arnold decided it was time to let someone else take the reins of the program. Judson's athletic director, Roy Wallace, had decided to retire, and wanted him to take his place. Arnold's chosen successor was Rutledge.

Parker and Rutledge would remain close through the years, but Parker was ready to be a head coach. Almost six hours away in the piney woods of East Texas, Parker got his shot at Marshall High School with the Mavericks.

Dennis Parker
Marshall High School was viewed as a bad job. It was in one of the toughest districts in the state. Its league included John Tyler, Lufkin, Nacogdoches, Pine Tree, Tyler Lee, Texas High, and Longview. In fact, the league was so competitive that Marshall hadn't won a playoff game since 1949. But football mattered in this region of the country. This was the community that produced Hall of Famer Y.A. Tittle of the New York Giants. The right person just needed to change the mindset.

Parker found out in a hurry just how bad morale had gotten when one of his new community members informed him about the upcoming season's expectations.

"A lady said to me, 'You're supposed to be a guy that can turn a program around,'" Parker recalled in an interview with *ArkLaTex.com*. "'So tell me how you know you've turned it around?'"

"I said, 'When you beat somebody you shouldn't have beaten,' and she replied, 'Well, you'll have ten chances next year.'"

Parker knew he would have to assess the younger players from the ground up. He needed to put a priority on the junior high system to have a pipeline of talent coming into the high school. A rigorous program meant hiring the right staff.

"When we were seventh-graders, it was Coach Parker's first year here and Marshall was not known as a big powerhouse program," said former player Shane Ford to *The Marshall News Messenger*.

Ford recalled that Parker "came to us and there were 133 of us in athletics, and he told us that if we did what he asked of us, we'd win a district title by the time we were seniors."

Parker didn't mince his words, telling Ford, "The problem with that is a lot of y'all won't be there. Look around because there will be about 30 of y'all left when all is said and done."

While his varsity position coaches and coordinators were well prepared from previous experience, Parker ended up adding three junior high coaches who would eventually enhance his legacy far greater than he'd ever imagined. The hires were Danny Long from California, Matt Turner from Iowa, and

Wayne Coleman from Missouri. The three out-of-staters were about to catch Texas high school football fever.

Danny Long

The Californian, Long, had been born in a small town in Oklahoma, and his family moved to Southern California before he entered high school. Once he'd joined the varsity team, he became a standout player, falling in love with football. After graduating, he attended a local community college and then took an offer to play for Bruce Snyder at Utah State.

"I fractured a disk in my lower back when I was at Utah State, and I went home, so I offered to help out my old high school coach," said Long. "I stayed in SoCal and ended up finishing my degree at Long Beach State."

Once he graduated, he took his first full-time coaching job at Rio Hondo Junior College in Whittier, California, but it wasn't long until Texas football caught his eye.

"I had a friend living in Texas at the time. He was working at Spring High School," Long said. "I flew down to see him over the Easter Break, and he took me around. I saw the Cy Fair stadium, and was amazed, so I came back to California and announced that I was moving to Texas."

Long got a job in the Humble Independent School District, a half hour drive from Houston, where Sam Mosley was the AD, but his time with Mosley was short lived. He stayed only a year and a half before taking a job in sales and marketing in New York. After a few office-bound years, he was itching to coach again, and he decided to look for the largest Texas town that was close to Shreveport, Louisiana. He called Coach Parker on the off chance that Parker had any openings or had heard of any in that area.

His timing was perfect. Parker was looking for a coach.

"Here's how much I wanted to get back in the game," he said. "After being a college coach, I took a job as a junior high coach at 30 years old."

He recalled, "I remember Parker would have us scout games on Friday nights, since we coached junior high on Thursdays. Doug Cox was the head coach at Longview, Maurice Cook was at Pine Tree, Dennis Alexander was at Daingerfield, James Cameron was at Kilgore, and Sleepy Reynolds was at Carthage. I just fell in love with East Texas football. I'd scout Longview and Lufkin and John Tyler."

Long knew he'd found his niche in life.

Matt Turner
Matt Turner's route to Marshall started in the Midwest. Growing up in Crescent, Iowa, Turner was a standout player, particularly in baseball. After high school, he stayed in the area and played at the local junior college before transferring to Arkansas State to play his last two years for the Indians. His love of athletics caught fire and he went into coaching, getting his first job at Marked Tree School District, about 35 miles southeast of Jonesboro, to stay near his future wife, Jill.

"After a year of us both being at the school, I took a job in Poplar Bluff, Missouri, working for a Texan named George Short, a guy from the San Antonio area, who'd coached with the likes of D.W. Rutledge, Dennis Parker, and Tom Thrower."

The mentorship by Short and his eulogies about Texas football impressed Turner.

After Turner had been in Poplar Bluff for two years, Short announced that he was ready to move back to San Antonio and told Turner, "If you want to try coaching in Texas, this might be the time to do it. There's a guy in Marshall, Texas, named Dennis Parker. He's just taken a job in the school district there."

Short's exact word stayed with Turner: "You'll learn it all. You'll start at the bottom, and you'll learn bottom up. If you eventually want to be a head coach, this is the guy to show you the ins and outs of it."

Although Turner and his wife didn't know a soul in Marshall, he took the job of assistant junior high coach and worked with both Parker and the head assistant coach, Danny Long, as well as with Wayne Coleman.

Wayne Coleman
About two hours north of Poplar Bluff, Missouri, Wayne Coleman grew up in the suburbs of St. Louis. A talented football player, he was recruited by Missouri Western State. After an injury, he transitioned to being a student assistant for the team, and then—when his coach got a job at Southern Arkansas—he followed him there in the summer of 1986 to be a GA.

"My wife and I were out there for a year and a half, and then we were expecting our first child. We needed real money, and I saw that Marshall High School had posted an opening for an English teacher," Coleman said. "My undergraduate degree was in English. The only caveat was that the position was teaching only, and I still wanted to coach, so I took the trip down to Texas to interview."

A woman in human resources, Patsy Smith, told Coleman that the job was his if he wanted it, and he explained that he still wanted to coach football, even if he was teaching a full schedule.

Smith wanted a new English teacher badly enough that she got Parker on the phone and told him that he had a new coach. Parker protested that he didn't have any openings.

"You do now," she said.

Coleman walked to the coaches' office to introduce himself.

"He was quick to inform me I was going to be an eighth-grade football coach. I went from coaching a DII All-American linebacker the previous season to coaching eighth grade football," Coleman said with a laugh.

All three coaches—Long, Turner, and Coleman—knew what they were signing on for.

"Dennis Parker is just like the Dallas Cowboys," said Long. "You either love him or you hate him, but one thing is for certain, it's a high accountability, and high responsibility job. On Mondays I hated it, on Tuesdays I loved it."

But these young coaches wanted to learn and weren't put off. Parker had been to the top of the mountain. Lesson one was "treat your staff well."

"I was the young guy who had coached at DII and had an All-American," said Coleman. "And I was offering up ideas all the time. I didn't know what I didn't know. I was the dumbest one in the room. But Dennis didn't talk down to anyone in front of the staff. He would let me go on and on and then say, 'No, we're not going to do that,' but he would tell me privately."

"He was so good about pulling me to the side, coaching me up. He helped me grow without turning me off to coaching. He really did believe that his most important coaches on the staff were his middle school coaches, so he invested in us, and he made sure that we felt important."

It soon became clear to the trio that Parker had a vision for the program that encapsulated more than just football. It was a mission of giving kids a sense of belonging and leading them to their peak performance.

"That's where I began to see, it was God who was trying to use me to make His difference in the role He was trying to lead me to," Turner said. "It was an exciting time too. Marshall hadn't had any significant success for many years, and they were hungry for it."

The first three years were rough.

From 1984 to 1986, the Mavericks had a combined record of 11-19. But in 1987, the team and the fans finally saw some fruits of the new staff's labor. The team won eight games, more than it had in over 20 years. And even though the team didn't qualify for the playoffs, it did finally beat a team it wasn't supposed to—Lufkin High School.

However, arch-rival and district champion Longview High School continued to have the Mavericks' number. By the time the 1987 season ended, Longview had extended its winning streak to 19 straight seasons.

"They used to have a saying," said former Marshall player, Dr. Chris Glanton, to *The Marshall News Messenger*. "There are three things you're sure of—death, taxes, and Longview beating Marshall."

Coleman understood the town's hunger to beat Longview.

"The townspeople have war wounds from taking those butt-kickings from Longview all those years," he said.

Parker knew how talented his team was going to be next year. It had the right supporting cast of tough, hard-nosed players coupled with extraordinary talent like senior running back Odell Beckham. They just needed to get over the mental hurdle that was Longview.

Parker decided to add a state-wide power to its non-district schedule so the team could play the best of the best. Odessa Permian was the standard for Texas high school football at the time. They had already won two 5A state championships in the 1980s with another state title game appearance to go with it.

"Once we scheduled Odessa Permian, everybody forgot about Longview," said Parker.

The game was on a Saturday to accommodate Permian's travel plans to Marshall.

Coleman recalled, "At Arkansas games, we might have 1,500 people total. But playing on our home field at Marshall that afternoon, the stadium was packed—you even had fans from Odessa there to see the teams play.

The crowd was even international. It included a group of Russian scientists.

"They were in the area dismantling nuclear missiles at a power plant, and they wanted to take in an American football game," said Coleman. "It was right at the end of the Cold War. They were wearing red and sitting in the end zone. It was crazy the appeal that game had."

Even crazier was that Odessa Permian hadn't lost a non-district game in years and the David in this match took down a Goliath. Given almost no chance to win the game by a skeptical state-wide media, Marshall won 13-12. The downtrodden community burst with pride over the victory.

"Even the Russians cheered wildly at the end of the game," Long said. "I was like gosh, we're going to have an international incident at a high school football game."

The Mavericks were a legitimate contender. By scheduling the game, it had served two important lessons that Parker wanted his team to learn. First, they were good enough to beat anyone. And second, he wanted them to see what a professional high school football program looked like. Permian was a model of sportsmanship as well as athleticism, lining up after the game to shake the Marshall players' hands.

"There was a certain amount of class they had," said Turner. "They knew about being their best. They had a different experience athletically in terms of their belief system. I remember thinking how much our team could learn from that."

That night the victory became even sweeter when the Marshall staff drove over to see another game to scout a future opponent.

"They announced it over the loudspeaker," said Parker, "and I almost couldn't believe my ears. 'This afternoon Odessa Permian 12, Marshall 13,' and the crowd went nuts. They were all for us."

Marshall continued its success, rattling off six straight wins, clinching at least a share of the district championship.

But one opponent still loomed, the Longview Lobos. And the Marshall locals saw the Lobos, under the direction of their new head coach, Robert Bero, as the team to beat.

"I was at East Texas Sporting Goods, and an older lady approached me and said, 'You're Coach Parker, right? Well, you ain't done nothing until you beat Longview, I don't care if you won district or not.'"

"I said, 'Yes, ma'am. I got you.'"

Marshall not only beat Longview, but they also absolutely blasted the Lobos, winning 28-0. Now the losing streak was over, and the old wounds could begin to heal.

The team continued its momentum beating its next two opponents to finish a perfect 10-0 on the season. Next, the Mavericks, won three successive playoff games. Still, they took nothing for granted and worked at their peak every practice knowing they were signed up to play Dallas Carter next, with Odessa Permian their likely opponent in the semifinals.

Carter had made headlines on the sports pages throughout much of the year. Extraordinarily talented, the team had 21 players who'd been offered college scholarships. Some state-wide pundits listed them as potentially one of, if not, the greatest Texas high school football team ever assembled. They were also in the news for an ongoing court battle between the school and the Texas Education Agency (TEA) over whether a grade had been changed for a player. The controversy was a distraction that overshadowed the team's success even though nothing had been officially ruled as of yet.

The game was evenly matched with Marshall narrowly leading towards the end of the game at Baylor's Floyd Casey Stadium. But on Carter's final drive, Robert Hall tossed a pass to Jessie Armstead in the closing seconds for the go-ahead touchdown. Marshall's incredible season was over.

Carter continued its dominance by beating Odessa Permian in the semifinals before taking down Parker's old team, Converse Judson, for the 5A state title.

But in a dramatic turn of post-season events, the TEA ruled against Carter High, claiming that a teacher had, in fact, illegally passed a player. The title was stripped away, and Converse Judson, led by Parker's friend, D.W. Rutledge, was crowned champion instead.

Marshall lay claim to a less exalted place in the record books. They were technically the only Texas high school to go undefeated, yet not win a state championship.

As a consolation prize, and in recognition of Marshall's turnaround and Parker's outstanding coaching, the UIL named him Texas's Coach of the Year.

"Coaches for some reason don't ever want to compare teams," said Parker. "I have no trouble saying that the '88 team was my best team ever."

The program was back and better than ever, and it was not slowing down.

In 1989, the Mavericks progressed one round further but ultimately lost in the semifinals to Odessa Permian, that year's state champion. However, the Marshall staff was recognized statewide for their excellent work and was selected to coach in the Texas High School All-Star Game that offseason. The extra time together was a built-in advantage for the following year, and they knew that they finally would be one of the favorites to win it all.

The next year brought a series of remarkable events. An obscure author from Philadelphia published a book about the season he spent with Odessa Permian's football team, *Friday Night Lights*. The story caught the public's imagination and became a cultural phenomenon of 1990. Suddenly, Texas high school football was in the spotlight, and that fame burnished the reputation of every high school football team in the state, from West Texas to Louisiana.

"I'm telling you, it was unbelievable," said Michael Epps, a former Marshall football player, in an interview with *The Marshall News Messenger*. "On Friday nights at Maverick Stadium, we filled the stands up. We were the NFL players of Marshall, Texas, and suddenly everybody was a Maverick."

The 1990 season was in the spotlight but started off sluggishly. After narrowly beating Louisiana's Monroe Wossman, the Mavericks dropped two of their next three games, including a lopsided 36-7 loss to Waco High.

"We hadn't really melded as a team because we were still moving around positions," said Truelove.

The path to the state title was going to get even steeper.

Earlier in the year, the UIL announced that Class 5A would break into two divisions for the first time ever, with a big school and a small school division. Marshall narrowly missed the cutoff for the small school division, and as one of the smallest schools in "Big 5A," they were dwarfed by district neighbors like Longview and Lufkin.

Ultimately, the change had no negative effect. Parker had built the program in his image, so the Mavericks were tough both physically and mentally. They regrouped from their slow start and won their next six games to capture their third consecutive district championship. The team was now led by a defense that had three first-team all-state players and a starting unit dubbed "The Red Brick Wall."

"We were the smallest school, but we went three years in a row and didn't lose a game in a district that had Longview, Lufkin, John Tyler," said Long.

The Mavericks advanced all the way to the state championship game with relative ease. The final match pitted them against Converse Judson. Dennis Parker would finally be going up against his old friend, D.W. Rutledge.

And this time Parker would get the best of him. In a dramatic showdown, Marshall held on to a 21-19 win over Judson after fumbling on the goal line and giving up a late touchdown. It was the first state championship in the town's history.

"The whole town was out in full force," said Truelove. "The overpasses were full of folks holding posters, it was pretty cool."

The moment was bittersweet, though. Moments before the game started, Parker had announced to his players that he had accepted the job as the new head coach for the University of North Texas. This would be his last game with the program.

Bill Harper, an internal candidate, was named Parker's replacement shortly after he left, but that didn't stop several of

Marshall's assistant coaches from also joining Parker at his new post. The Mavericks were about to look very different from a leadership standpoint.

Inspired by Parker's moxie, Danny Long decided to go out on his own, too.

"I interviewed for five or six places and didn't get the job," said Long. "Waskom, Brookshire Royal, Queen City. Then the Jacksonville job opened, and Walter Harris [the superintendent] and Dick Stone [the mayor and a school board member] decided to take a chance on a hot-shot O-line coach with all of the answers."

A roadblock appeared unexpectedly. Although Harris and Stone wanted him, the school board was conflicted about Long and questioned his qualifications. After all, they pointed out, he wasn't a coordinator. To make matters worse, there was another candidate, a staffer, with an inside edge. It looked like Long would lose the opportunity—but not for long.

"At the final board meeting, who comes walking down the hallway but Dennis Parker," said Long.

"He told the board what I'd done to help get the Mavericks the state championship. It was a 6:00 AM meeting, so he'd left Denton at 3:00 AM to make it."

"Dennis Parker is like the Dallas Cowboys. And I love the Dallas Cowboys."

Parker ruled the day, and Long got his job. A former salesman, he immediately went into pitch mode to build his staff, convincing and cajoling young coaches to come aboard. By then it was July, and he needed to act quickly.

Recalled Wayne Coleman, "There was a little concern that maybe Dennis had handpicked the top two or three assistants to go with him, and there was some concern over Marshall. So Danny offered me the OC job, and then he said, 'Can you talk Matt into coming?'"

Long had always thought of Matt Turner as the X factor, and he knew how much value he would instantly bring.

"So I remember I invited Matt and his family to our daughter's birthday," said Coleman, "I spent the entire day trying to convince him to go with us."

It was the worst time to leave because Turner had just bought a house, but the offer was too tempting to dismiss and, after a few days thought, he accepted Long's offer.

"In retrospect, that birthday party was pretty important to our future trajectories," said Coleman. "Of course, at the time, we had no idea what we'd started."

The following frame hangs in Danny Long's office. It is a nod to Marshall being one of the smallest schools in all of 5A, yet still winning the title. (Courtesy of Danny Long)

McLane Carter (#4) and Blake Lynch (#9) embrace in the end zone after a Gilmer touchdown. Carter had lost his best friend, Desmond Pollard, before the season began, and Lynch, who transferred into Gilmer without knowing anyone else on the team, quickly became one of Carter's closest friends. (Courtesy of Ruel Felipe)

"Blake was such a quiet performer. He never said anything while he played, was always very polite. He was freaky though."
--Todd Barr

Chapter 5: The Transfer

The 2013-2014 school year finally came to a close after a whirlwind two months for the players, coaches, and families of the Gilmer Buckeyes after the loss of Desmond Pollard.

The summer was a time for renewal and a chance for Buckeye players to get fired up to strengthen their game. And no one was better at pouring gasoline on that fire than Jeff Traylor.

"Coach Traylor ran summer workouts like a college program," said McLane Carter. "It was a *program*. They were prolonged workouts that were well-designed and awesome."

The Gilmer players who had come of age in Traylor's program knew what to expect, but the newbies to the program were blindsided by the intensive pace and conditioning.

One new student stood out, though, because he embraced the challenge.

Before transferring to Gilmer, Blake Lynch had been the star quarterback for Troup High School, located about 50 miles south of Gilmer. Already committed to Art Briles and the Baylor Bears, Lynch had established himself as one of the best players ever to come out of the school. Competing in Class 3A, Troup was a small town with just under 2,000 residents, and Blake's talent was obvious from the get-go.

"The first time I met Blake was when he was in the fourth grade," said former Troup coach Olan Johnson. "I remember a little bitty boy with braids shooting in the gym with some of his friends and I asked who he was because even though he was tiny you could tell that he was going to be a dude someday."

Blake realized that potential and then some.

As a high school sophomore, he'd led Troup Tigers football to a 9-2 record and captured a share of the district championship. As a junior, he made the playoffs again, even though he was injured for part of the year. By the start of his senior year, everyone expected that he'd lead the Tigers to another championship. But there was trouble brewing on the home front, and that trouble was Blake's stepfather.

In the middle of divorce, Blake's mother feared her husband, with good reason, and she was determined to get herself and her kids out of town. At first the family considered moving to Tyler, the nearest city, but Mrs. Lynch wanted to resettle in a small town, and she chose Gilmer. Moving had one downside, though. Blake was a star quarterback player about to enter his senior year and moving meant cutting short his career at Troup. The move was risky, but Blake was about to have one of his most trusted mentors back in his life.

***

A son of Gilmer, Olan Johnson had grown up as the middle child in a house with five kids, and sports, especially football, was his outlet. As a freshman, he made the varsity team as wide receiver and was on the path to a great second season until his plans were suddenly derailed the summer before his sophomore year, when he was in a car wreck.

"I had to have a metal plate in my head, and I didn't get to play sports that entire school year. It killed me because sports was all I could think about," he said.

During his time away from the field, he developed the poise and patience that would distinguish him in the years to come. After finally returning to the Buckeyes as a junior, he transitioned to the quarterback position and led the team to a 5-5 record, a disappointing season performance. The district wanted new talent to ramp up the team's wins, and they got exactly that in 31-year-old Jeff Traylor.

"We would have run through a brick wall for him. He was that inspiring," said Johnson.

Traylor and his quarterback bonded quickly, and the coach brought the team to new heights with their first winning season in three years. Johnson's outstanding performance springboarded him into college ball, playing first for Navarro in Corsicana and then for Texas College in Tyler.

But being a pro player wasn't his dream, being an inspiring coach in the mold of Jeff Traylor was.

"The impact that Coach Traylor had on me made me want to come back home someday and have the same effect on other kids," he said.

After he graduated from Texas College, Johnson wanted to earn his coaching chops before someday returning to Gilmer, so he took a job working for John Eastman at Troup High School.

All the while, Traylor had been recruiting Johnson to work for him, but the timing didn't feel right. Finally, after eight years under the tutelage of three different head coaches, including

Hall of Famer Dennis Alexander, he felt seasoned enough to return to Gilmer.

"I wanted to represent my hometown," he said.

***

When Blake Lynch called his former Troup coach to let him know about his planned move to Gilmer, Johnson worried about the optics.

"I told him, whoa man, people are going to think you're coming here for me," said Johnson. "As soon as I finished talking with him, I called Dennis Alexander and told him that Blake was thinking about coming to Gilmer. Dennis understood that Blake wasn't leaving Troup for athletics but for survival. Dennis was more concerned about the situation with Blake's stepfather than with the impact on his team."

Unfortunately, this explanation about the transfer never made it to the red-hot message boards of East Texas high school football coaches and fans. When Lynch showed up to enroll at Gilmer, they blasted Traylor and his staff.

"Jeff always did everything by the book," said Kerry Lane, a young coach on Traylor's staff. "Every year, people take shots at Gilmer because of players moving in. People never talk about the kids who leave here and play at other places, though."

"This was his momma's decision," said Kurt Traylor. "She picked Gilmer because her family needed a safe place to live. Saying that we cheat is such a lazy point of view. 'They must be cheating.' Naw, they're working. We didn't *have* to recruit at Gilmer. Kids *wanted* to play for us."

"We knew we hadn't done anything wrong," said Gilmer coach Alan Metzel. "There was sincerity there."

Traylor made sure his staff stayed focused on the task at hand rather than get confrontational with critics. It helped that this wasn't the first time that football fans had put a target on the Buckeyes' backs.

In the summer of 2006, Traylor had endured similar wrath when star player G.J. Kinne had transferred in from Canton High School just before his senior year. Like Blake, G.J. was dealing with violence. Gary Joe Kinne—Canton's head coach—had been shot at point blank range in his office by the irate father of one of his players, and his family wanted to leave town and move to Gilmer.

"Everything had been checked off for G.J., but two superintendents voted against a transfer, even with a kid whose father had just been shot. It was a 2-2 vote, and it had to go to UIL to make the final decision, and they signed off on it," Traylor said.

"I got killed by other coaches when G.J. moved in—by haters—but it is what it is," he said.

In Blake's case, Traylor made sure to tune out the criticism.

"I wasn't going to listen to the noise this time, and I even banned *Smoaky* from the fieldhouse."

Smoaky was an online high school sports forum that started in 2001 by the famous Texas sportscaster, David Smoak. Smoak was the premier voice in East Texas sports from 1990-2009 before expanding into the Central Texas region. The online forum he created is an integral part of the high school sports culture that makes regions like East Texas so special. Everyone has a voice and no topic is off limits. And almost everyone who lives in towns like Gilmer and Troup has an opinion.

Despite the hubbub around Blake, Dennis Alexander signed his transfer paper because he cared about his player first and foremost.

"I love Coach A," Blake said years later. "I know he didn't want one of his best players leaving, but he wanted what was best for me and my family."

Yet, as much as Blake wanted to play for Gilmer, the transfer held potential risks for his career. Gilmer was loaded, and Blake would have to earn his spot and learn a new culture.

"You know, Gilmer had been a powerhouse for like the last 14 to 15 years," he said. "I honestly didn't know anything about the team before moving there."

Blake may not have known about the Buckeyes, but the Gilmer coaches knew all about him, and those who didn't started to pay attention in a hurry.

"That kid could *play*," said Kerry Lane. "Before you know it, he started showing up at the workouts, and we all were watching him in the first seven-on-seven practices. He ran downfield and caught a deep ball perfectly. We were like, 'Well, alright.'"

"When he jumped on the field and busted his ass, that's when our other kids said, 'Ok. He's one of us. He can do it,'" said Kurt. "Because there's a lot of them that won't do it, and they disappear. 'This is too much, Coach.' These guys here have done it since sixth grade – they know the culture. Blake's dedication earned their respect."

Looking back on those days, Lynch recalled, "I wasn't like a Hollywood DI athlete that thought he had made it. I was trying to grind like everybody else. I wanted to compete and after a couple of practices, either Kris or McLane said, 'Hey, you can play a little bit.' The discipline and structure of the program were such a blessing for me, and we were essentially playing at a college level under Coach Traylor."

Olan Johnson remembers that Blake came in and "picked up the offense and defense so quickly."

By the end of a backbreaking summer training with a two-a-day format, Blake had established himself as someone who belonged and could contribute. The final piece in integrating into the team would be the way the former Troup star handled his relationships with the Buckeyes two best players and team leaders, Kris Boyd and McLane Carter.

"He and Kris had some battles," said Lane. "I remember that Kris pressed Blake one time on the track when he was covering him and basically let him know that this ain't Troup."

"Me and Kris would bump heads early on since I was a receiver, and he was one of the top corners in the state. But at the end of the day, it was all love. We just wanted to make each other better," Blake said.

The two competitors had similar skill sets but played different positions. In contrast, Carter was a quarterback, the same position Blake had played at Troup.

"My junior year there, I ended up breaking my arm and wrist during the season," Blake said. "Coming off my surgery, I couldn't really throw the ball like I wanted to. To be honest, McLane Carter threw the ball better than me, and he was a better fit to play quarterback on that team."

"McLane was just the general, too. We had so many different personalities. He was the only guy on our team that could mesh everybody together. He ended up being one of my best friends and still is to this day."

Traylor and his staff had an eagle eye for identifying talent, and they always found the best way to use it. Although Lynch wasn't the starting quarterback, he became a weapon that showed up to play receiver, running back, and, sometimes, quarterback when they ran the wildcat formation.

"Jeff would find a safety that was on the third-string, and he'd go over to the D-line coach and say, 'Can we get nine reps with him here, because he's quick,'" said Metzel. "He's also very much a visionary, a big picture guy. He can always see three to four steps down the road."

Metzel recalled that when he was working on quarterbacks, Jeff would look over at what he was doing and push him harder and motivate him with lines like, "When we play Cuero round four, is that going to beat them?"

"I'd say, 'Well, I haven't thought of that,' and Jeff's like, 'We have to be thinking about how we beat Cuero and Argyle.' He's always thinking ahead," Metzel recalled.

"He walked me through the entire season before our first game, and, no lie, he predicted every playoff game that we would play," said Carter.

The 2014 season began with the Gilmer Buckeyes taking on the Liberty-Eylau Leopards in Tyler's Rose Stadium as the marquee matchup in the annual Trinity Mother Francis Football Classic.

"East Texas Football under the lights at Tyler Rose Stadium," said Carter. "Tough to beat that kind of opener."

That night, Carter and Boyd took full advantage of their opportunities to light up the scoreboard. Boyd caught three touchdown passes from Carter and spent the majority of the night lined up at receiver to take advantage of obvious mismatches. Carter went on to have five touchdown passes total for the evening, and Gilmer cruised to a 55-16 season-opening win.

"It felt like we were playing some big-time football," said Carter. "We were fresh out of summer camp, and we handed it to LE. We're like, 'This is going to be a lot of fun.'"

Lynch, on the other hand, made his Buckeye debut by touching the ball only three times. All three touches went for touchdowns. One of them was a 54-yard touchdown run on Gilmer's second play from scrimmage.

"I think that was the moment that the coaches and players realized, 'Hey, we need to get this guy the ball,'" said Lynch.

"Blake was such a quiet performer," said Todd Barr. "He never said anything while he played, was always very polite. He was freaky though."

"I think I kind of took for granted how good he was because I'd see him every day at Troup," added Johnson. "And then he comes to Gilmer and for him to do the things he was doing, that's when he really stood out."

The timing of this new union between Lynch and the Buckeyes was crucial for both sides after the death of their beloved senior, Pollard, the year before.

"Don't get me wrong, he did not take the place of Dez," said Kurt Traylor. "But it was like the good Lord said, *Hey, you lost a player, but you're going to gain another one that's going to affect you guys just as much.* He was such a blessing to be around—and he was so coachable."

"Gilmer accepted me and my family with open arms," said Lynch. "Most seventeen- and eighteen-year-olds wouldn't like someone coming in and potentially getting some of their touches or scoring touchdowns. They had an established group that had been together since they were like eleven years old. And they still accepted me. I just really appreciated that."

Players knew what it was like to be in Blake's shoes. His narrative was similar to the stories of a lot of the guys on the team. He didn't come from money, and his mom was the leader of the house. In a sense, the team came to act as the type of family that so many of them longed for.

"Our program is crucial for young men in our community," said Keith Tate. "Just having fourteen or fifteen coaches checking on kids and loving them outside of sports. A lot of them don't have men at home, so there are some things that we have to teach them that's outside of football."

Under Traylor, Buckeye coaches gladly played that role.

"That's one of Traylor's big mantras right there," said Kerry Lane. "Do not sit in the coaches' office. Be with the kids. They need to know that we see them as more than just players on the field."

"Every coach in America wants the kids to buy into what they're doing. Well, you have to buy into *them* first. It has to be more than about football. You need to know them, and their mommas, and where they go to church. Everybody says that and still most coaches will just go and sit in their office after practice. Doing that we don't teach kids how to trust us."

"There are so many kids who don't have a father figure nowadays," said long-time Gilmer resident Pete Herrmann. "One thing that I always respected about Jeff Traylor was that when he got hired here, he brought in the Adopt-a-Buckeye program."

The Adopt-a-Buckeye program was in its 15th year as a part of the overall football program. The initiative connected members of the community with current football players to be a kind of extended family to them.

"When we first started the Adopt-a-Buckeye Program, it was big time," said Jeff Traylor. "We had a lot of kids who didn't have parents that were able to come to their games. All I did was challenge everybody in the community to pick one player and write them a card once a week, and then be there when the game was over to talk with them about how they did. Now, almost every kid in Gilmer has two to three 'parents' that adopt them. After the game, it's like a huge family reunion on the field."

"It really builds that bridge for football and community members," said Brian Bowman. "My wife and I have done it for years. It's just simple stuff really, a card or a candy bar or a goodie bag. It's not necessarily what the gift is. It's that someone in the community is taking time out of their schedule to care about you."

Traylor and his staff also knew that this kind of support was crucial for a team getting ready to go through a difficult stretch. The non-district schedule was going to be tough, and it was strategically designed to test the Buckeyes early. Just two weeks after the LE game, the Buckeyes would face a three-game stretch where they would go up against the three most dominant East Texas programs of the last 20 years—the Tatum Eagles, the Daingerfield Tigers, and the Carthage Bulldogs.

A young Jeff Traylor (standing in the center next to head coach Danny Long) joins Jacksonville's coaching staff and begins getting mentored by Wayne Coleman and Matt Turner (pictured in front of Traylor). (Courtesy of Cari Traylor)

Jeff Traylor and Danny Long pictured together before a Jacksonville football game. (Courtesy of Danny Long)

"Danny called me, and I took the job over the phone. I'd never even met him in person."
--Jeff Traylor

Chapter 6: The Proving Ground

In July of 1991, three coaches, and friends, agreed to take on the large task of transforming Jacksonville High School into a winner. Danny Long, Wayne Coleman, and Matt Turner had worked together at high-riding Marshall High School, and their goal was to recreate the same kind of magic that was present at their previous stop.

Long arrived in Jacksonville first with the mandate of turning the Jacksonville Indians around after a dismal 5-5 season. He hit the ground running, knowing that his success rode on assembling a talented coaching staff. At Marshall, he'd worked with coaches he considered the best in the region, and now he wanted them by his side, so he brought in former colleague Wayne Coleman as offensive coordinator. He also wanted another Marshall coach, Matt Turner, on offense, but Turner was initially nowhere to be found.

"I got the job in late July, and Matt had gone to Minnesota during the summer vacation to see his brother, so I couldn't get in touch with him," said Long. "When he finally returned to Marshall, our head coach, Dennis Parker, had gone to North Texas and taken a lot of the Marshall staff with him. I honestly think Matt went into a meeting and looked around and saw that all his guys had left. So, he called me and asked if there was room for him at Jacksonville—and I told him, 'Lord, yes!'"

Long knew exactly what kind of structures he wanted to put in place, and he went to work advocating for his coaches with the high school's administration.

"Danny set us up for success. He got our teaching assignments figured out well. He also got parents to buy in right away, telling them that he'd do things the Marshall way," said Coleman.

"You have to remember that Danny was a car salesman before he was a coach. He never claimed to be the greatest football mind, but he knew he was a great salesman, and he got the town behind us."

Jacksonville is a blue-collar East Texas town outside of Tyler. Its population is about 60 percent White, 20 percent Black, and 20 percent Hispanic, and many people worked at the small plants and pallet mills that skirted the town, a diverse group that united around the activities of the local school district, especially its football and basketball teams.

"He really had a vision for building a program in the mold of our Marshall head coach, Dennis Parker," said Turner. "We went into it thinking it would be a matter of just replicating what we'd known—but it wasn't that simple. There's just a lot more to it than that."

In fact, the first year was humbling. Long, Coleman, and Turner faced the harsh reality that they'd left jobs where they were regular district champions to going 2-8 in their first year in Jacksonville. But Long knew Jacksonville's storied history, and he also knew they could bring the crowds back to the Indians' stadium, dubbed the "Tomato Bowl," if they could catch a ray of their past glory.

***

The Tomato Bowl was synonymous with the Jacksonville community. The gateway to the stadium entrance was built with red iron ore rocks unearthed from the land of local farmers then hewn into giant stones to create a colossal wall that also surrounded the press box and the home-side stands. The bowl's history stretched back to 1938, the tail end of the Great Depression and the prelude to World War II. Even in hard times, the district had secured $100,000 to build a stadium to rival any in the state and hired a fancy Dallas architect to design it. In a testament to the project's great success, the Tomato Bowl still houses the Indians and is just the fifth stadium in all of Texas history to be designated a Texas Football Hall of Fame Stadium.

A legendary stadium needs a legendary coach, and one truly worthy of the Tomato Bowl arrived in 1958, the twelfth in a succession of Jacksonville coaches. Bum Phillips came to Jacksonville via Division I powerhouse Texas A&M. There, he'd been assistant coach to future Hall of Famer Paul "Bear" Bryant for just a year before Bryant was successfully wooed away by the University of Alabama to be its head coach.

Bum Phillips was quite the hire for Jacksonville, and he brought in equally impressive talents. Shortly after he arrived there, Phillips convinced a good friend, Dick Sheffield, to leave his head coaching post at Beaumont High and work by his side. East Texas lore has it that Sheffield was persuaded by Phillips casting a vision that Sheffield would also be living in a nice property atop rolling hills with grazing cows and hunting dogs, the whole nine yards. That vision didn't last long for the two friends. Just one year later, Phillips took a head coaching job at another school, eventually moving three more times before landing as an NFL head coach for the Houston Oilers. Sheffield always declined to join his friend on his coaching journey and instead chose to stay in Jacksonville and serve the community as its head coach. Just two years after Phillips left, Sheffield powered the Indians to their first undefeated regular season.

"Sheffield was such a good man," said long-time Jacksonville resident, Pat McCown. "Now, he was hard! I told him that I was 40 years old before I quit being scared of him. He really was one of a kind, though. Very devout Christian. Taught Sunday School. Just a good man."

Sheffield remained in his post for another decade and stayed on in Jacksonville after he retired. It had become his family's home.

By the time Long arrived in 1991, the Indians had been floundering for years, much to the disappointment of their fans. One particularly dismayed group was a group of grown men who had once played under Sheffield and continued to idolize him. These former players' sons were the new generation of Indians, whom Long would be coaching, often under the watchful gaze of their fathers.

What they saw impressed them. Long and Sheffield shared a similar philosophy of toughening up their teams with boot-camp-style training. For Sheffield this had meant, in addition to other backbreaking methods, strapping 20-pound sandbags on his players' backs and making them run uphill. Long called his version of the boot camp the "Indian Maker."

"I remember going out and seeing them in practice doing some crazy stuff," said Pat McCown, one of the football dads who had played under Sheffield. "It was the toughest stuff I'd seen. I called my old teammates and said, 'Guys, we're getting ready to win again, because this guy is crazier than Dick.'"

Also, like Sheffield, Long knew how to rally a community and promote his team. He created the Adopt-an-Indian program, which enlisted local men to "adopt" football players and mentor them. Long insisted that his players dress up on game days and wear a white dress shirt and tie to school, bringing a new touch of class to the team.

"We had a lot of sizzle with our program," said Long. "We did stuff like that to make it a special atmosphere. Some people say that kids don't want to do that anymore. That's a lie. Yes, they do. It's an honor to get to be on varsity, go to a pep rally, and learn how to tie a necktie. I'm a big believer that we're supposed to prepare kids for life. They need to be playing for something bigger than themselves."

***

McCown was a big supporter of Long, and his largest contribution to the team was his son, Randy, a talented quarterback and one of three McCown boys who were standout athletes. (His brothers, Josh and Luke, also coached by Long, became NFL players.)

Randy, already a star in basketball, joined the football team at the start of his sophomore year, Long's second year at Jacksonville.

During his first season, the coach had been experimenting with the veer, a ball control offense that had been popularized across Texas by Bill Yeoman, a Hall-of-Famer who'd coached the Houston Cougars for more than two decades.

In his second season, with Randy McCown now as his roster, Long finally started to change his ways. In a lopsided game against Corsicana, Jacksonville was down by several touchdowns, and Long decided to give his offensive architects, Coleman and Turner, the green light to turn their young prodigy loose. McCown responded by lighting up the scoreboard with his passing ability and almost pulled off an impossible comeback.

"That game changed the culture of the program," said Pat McCown.

It was a morale booster for the young quarterback and the team, but, even more important, it was confirmation to Long that they could be innovative with the passing game. Putting the icing on the cake, the elder McCown delivered with his vote of confidence, sweetening a town that was starved of football glory.

***

Pat McCown, the family patriarch, played football for Jacksonville in high school, but claims that he was "nothing special."

His father owned and ran M&H manufacturing, a small pallet mill that employed around ten to twelve people when Pat was a young boy.

"My family has been in the lumber, timber, and pallet business for forever," said McCown. "Once you get sawdust in your veins, you can't get it out."

When Pat took over M&H, he grew it into a 200-person operation with three locations across East Texas. Pat's wife, Robin, was his high school sweetheart and she worked just as hard as her husband. She taught fifth and sixth grade Science for 30 years in New Summerfield, a modest community just outside of Jacksonville. Both parents, Jacksonville residents to this day, instilled the value of hard work in their children: Randy, his two brothers, and his sister, Amy. Today, they have eighteen grandchildren, including eleven grandsons and seven granddaughters.

"The entire family, just the quality of people they are, they're just amazing," said Matt Turner. "They would say it's Christ because they were really strong in their faith. I probably learned more from that family than they did from me. Pat used to say that God smiled on their family."

Growing up with parents who expected excellence, Randy gave the Indians his all, and, with him on the roster and Long in charge, the team looked forward to a winning season.

***

Always eager to make his organization better, Long knew he needed to add another quality varsity assistant, so he looked up a man who knew East Texas football like the back of his hand, Ken Jones.

Jones was a sales rep for East Texas Sporting Goods. In that close-knit region, the reps weren't just a sales force; they were a brotherhood of former coaches—including former Indians coach Dick Sheffield—and the coaches' many compadres. The network of reps traveled from town to town selling to schools and, while they just happened to be there, sizing up all the coaches and players they saw. In a pre-Google era, the reps collectively served as the database for high school football: the stats, the teams, and the fields. In a football-crazed land, they wielded outsized influence, making and breaking careers.

"The sporting goods reps are like the mafia," said Long. "When the mafia tells you to interview someone, I knew I was going to likely hire them."

Long knew that Ken Jones had an unrivaled knowledge of East Texas football, so he connected with him through Sheffield.

"Ken kept telling me about this guy from Big Sandy named Jeff Traylor," Long recalled. "He tells me that Jeff needs to come work for me," said Long.

Big Sandy High School had once been the dominant school in East Texas. Coached by Jim Norman in the 1970s, the Wildcats had won three straight state championships from 1973 to 1975 and produced the likes of NFL head coach Lovie Smith and NFL player David Overstreet.

Traylor had just completed his fourth year at Big Sandy when Long reached out to him.

"Danny called me, and I took the job over the phone," said Traylor. "In fact, we never even met in person before he hired me, but I did finally meet up with him in San Angelo at a clinic that summer."

Traylor was hired as an assistant football and basketball coach. His teaching assignment was World History, and, as the low man on the totem pole, he also helped coach the junior high sports programs and whatever else the others didn't want to do.

When he arrived at Jacksonville, "Danny was the only one I knew, and that was from the interview. Talk about a risk—but it paid off," said Traylor. "I was coaching varsity and junior high school, but deep down I had an ambition to be a head coach one day, and I think Danny knew that and respected it. Getting to go to Jacksonville to work with him, Matt, and Wayne was the gamechanger in my career."

***

The risk Jeff took was especially great because he had a wife, Cari, and a nine-month-old baby, Jordan.

"Jeff got a call from Danny Long asking if he wanted to come to Jacksonville. We were both so excited, both of us jumping on the bed, ecstatic. We left the next month," said Cari Traylor.

"We lived at a couple different places during our time at Big Sandy. Our last year we lived in this yellow house off the highway that we called the Yellow Love Shack. It had a window unit, just a very temporary place. I thought Jacksonville would be a great place for a growing family to flourish, and I was right."

Jeff and Cari had met when they were students at Stephen F. Austin State University and they both worked as lifeguards at the local pool. The meeting was more than serendipity.

"How Jeff tells it is that his friend told him that his future wife was working at the pool," said Cari. "Jeff says he saw me, and then he decided he needed to be working there, too."

After graduating from Stephen F. Austin, Jeff started coaching at Big Sandy, and he and Cari wed after a quick engagement.

"Being from Houston, I didn't think I could live in such a small town right off the bat, and I told Jeff that I thought we needed to live in Tyler," said Cari. "It was a 30-minute drive to Big Sandy, and he was okay with that. But I had no idea about the crazy schedule he'd have and the long hours. He'd work all day and then have the drive home when he was exhausted. That's not safe. So, after a year we decided to move to Gilmer, which is half the distance."

Big Sandy was a revolving door of coaches. In four years, Traylor worked for three different head coaches, endured two 0-10 seasons, and had zero playoff appearances. He did get a chance to show his value though. During his fourth year, under new head coach Darold Turner, Traylor was promoted to offensive coordinator, and the Wildcats won six games, which was their highest total in 10 years.

In addition to his time on the football field, he was spending hours getting valuable experience as the head basketball coach.

"I was the head basketball coach my last three years," said Traylor. "Coach McGinnis gave me that assignment. We were young and won nine my first year, thirteen my second, and then won seventeen my last year."

Coaching basketball would come in handy later for Traylor. The lessons he learned on spacing and ball movement would directly impact his offensive philosophy later in his football coaching —but, ultimately, Big Sandy, with its rapid turnover, didn't seem like the place to build that career.

He was ripe for change when Long called him about the Jacksonville job, and Cari loved the community she began building in Jacksonville.

"It was our first real coaching family," she said. "Maybe it's because we spent more time there. It was my first time to look at coaching families and how much we all have in common. As big of a character as Danny is, his wife was just the cutest and sweetest thing. She was kind to everyone. Just being there so long and hanging out, going through the same kinds of things, that was a good dose of the nice side of coaching families."

Her professional life flourished, too.

"I was working with a dual language program that was cutting edge for East Texas at the time," she said. "My son even attended. We got to travel a lot and see places that I normally wouldn't have gotten to see, and I worked with some great people. It was my favorite part of my career."

Like Cari, Jeff thrived in his job.

"When Jeff came, he made an immediate impact," said Long. "He was so young and positive. He had this old Camaro, and he would load kids up in his car and go play pickup basketball with them. Kids loved him."

As Jeff recalls, Long put him to work at once.

"Danny gave me every job that he didn't want," said Traylor laughing. "Equipment, special teams, quarterbacks, receivers, DBs. He told me it was because he thought it would help me be a great head coach one day."

"Danny is as good with people as I've ever seen. He can sell ice to an Eskimo. He's the best at making you believe that it was your idea when it was his. Truthfully, I think he just loved working me to death."

Traylor's basketball savvy soon came in handy for recruiting the best athletes. Jacksonville was a big basketball town with well-respected teams at two local colleges, Lon Morris and Jacksonville College. Traylor knew basketball culture and quickly established a rapport with the basketball players at

Jacksonville High School—relationships that benefitted the football program directly.

"Sure enough, we started having the kids who'd played straight basketball play football, too," Long said. "This was a direct influence of Jeff's relationships with those kids."

Like the school, the community had a personal stake in the team, especially in Randy McCown, who improved every year, and, under the staff's tutelage, was rising through the ranks of high school quarterbacks to become one of the best in the state. But even a talent of his magnitude couldn't carry an entire team, and the 1994 season finished with a 5-5 record.

"That didn't go over really well with the community," said Traylor. "Everyone expected so much from Randy. If we knew what we know now, we could've done so much better as coaches. We were all young, still trying to figure it all out."

McCown's talent gained widespread attention. He made *Dave Campbell Magazine's* All-Super Team and accepted a scholarship to play for R.C. Slocum at Texas A&M. Three years later as the Aggies starter, he would lead his team to the school's only Big 12 Championship and a BCS Bowl appearance.

***

Just as Jeff was a mentor, he found mentors in the talented coaches surrounding him. Wayne Coleman served as a big brother figure to Traylor and was especially helpful in advising him how to cope with Long's drive and intensity. Dick Sheffield had taken an immediate liking to Traylor and was a role model both on the field and at Central Baptist Church, where they both worshipped.

"He was an unbelievable Christian man," said Traylor. "And he was also a wealth of knowledge. He and Bum Phillips had been roommates together at Lamar. And, sure enough, every time Bum got a new job, even in the NFL, he always tried to hire Dick."

But the single greatest influence in Traylor's life was Matt Turner.

"After that first year, Matt sat me down and told me I was the greatest motivator he had ever seen, and that kids—Black, White, Hispanic—were drawn to me. He saw my strengths, but he also saw my weaknesses. He told me flat out, 'You don't know a damn thing about football, and you think you know everything. If you'll just shut your mouth for one year and listen, I'll make you the greatest Texas high school football coach ever.'"

Turner spoke frankly because he felt strongly.

"Jeff had a God-given ability, and you could see that," said Turner. "There was a lot he didn't know. Jeff is a talker, and he was a young coach at the time. He almost couldn't get out of his own way. It was just a matter of saying, 'Hey, I can help you if you'll let me.' To his credit, a lot of people would have taken that the wrong way. He understood it, and he ran with it."

The two men became incredibly close, and the relationship extended outside of football. They both had sons who were the same age, and both were devout Christians. Turner invited Traylor to Promise Keepers, a men's ministry founded by former University of Colorado head football coach Bill McCartney to help men to lead lives of integrity.

Traylor came to respect Turner so much that he even named his second child Jacob Matthew Traylor after Matthew Turner. He credits Turner with giving him the tools to be a great coach, including meticulous preparation.

"Matt has a process, a list, and he checks it off," explained Long. "And we're not leaving until he gets his stuff checked off. He doesn't want to fraternize, and he thinks sleep is the biggest waste of time. We used to ride in the van together on the way to San Angelo, and he'd fall asleep with a pen and pad in his hand."

Turner wanted only two things: to teach his players the game of football and then turn them into young men.

"Even if a kid is the worst player, Matt was going to coach him the same as the starters," said Coleman. "It's amazing. It irritates other coaches on the staff. They're thinking, 'Why are we giving this kid an extra rep when we should be getting the starters more reps?'"

Turner not only treated his players equally during practices but also was fair to them in delegating time off the bench, even during critical plays. When the other coaches questioned his decision, Turner would tell them, "That kid came to practice and worked his butt off just like everyone else."

"And if the kid actually made a catch, Matt would get on the headset and say, 'That's why we practice, boys!'" said Coleman.

Pat McCown also praised Matt and regarded him as the greatest coach his sons ever had.

"I remember when my youngest son was playing for the Cleveland Browns. The offensive coordinator asked about former coaches he'd really connected with prior to joining them," said McCown.

"Well, then I told him that the best football coach in the United States is a 3A offensive coordinator named Matt Turner. I don't think he expected to hear that. But it was true."

Unlike Turner, Long was a stern taskmaster with Traylor, to the point where it could be counterproductive.

"I tried to be the tough, crusty boss, because I had seen that modeled by Dennis Parker," said Long. "Dennis was incredibly hard on me, so I thought that was the best way to do it, and I was incredibly hard on Jeff. I thought if I was hard on the coaches in practice, then the kids would respond because they didn't want their coach to get chewed out."

Traylor didn't appreciate this at the time, but later in life had an appreciation for what his boss was trying to do.

"I was Danny's whipping boy that first year," said Traylor. "I thought I was smarter than him, so I probably deserved it. I needed to be knocked down."

"Jeff isn't like that with his players and coaches though," said Long. "Looking back, if I went back into coaching again, I would probably try to be more like him."

Wayne Coleman helped Traylor deal with Long.

"When Danny was all over me, Wayne would talk me off a cliff," said Traylor.

"It was different because me and Matt were with Danny at Marshall, and we'd all worked under Dennis and knew the drill," said Coleman. "But Jeff took it hard early on. He wanted to quit."

"In the coaches dressing room one day, I remember Jeff saying, 'I'm not doing this anymore. I'm done,' and I said, 'No, you're not. What you're going to do is quit listening to him. You're going to let him yell all he wants. Just let it slide right off. You notice how he doesn't yell at me and Matt. It's because we don't listen to the shouting.'"

After a pep talk, Traylor would tell Coleman, "I think I can finish the season," and Coleman would reassure him, "You're going to be fine."

The relationship between Traylor and Long took a turn for the better when Traylor began to prove himself.

"Jeff became my eyes and ears," said Long. "We'd talk about ways to improve the program non-stop. I remember we'd stay up late talking on the phone about Bill Parcells's book *Finding a Way to Win*. Jeff was about 10 years younger than me, so he was a jolt in my veins. He was an unbelievable assistant coach."

By 1995, Long had been coaching for four years. Although the team had yet another hard season, going 3-7, Long's staff was confident that they were headed in the right direction. They were becoming smarter. They were gelling together. And they had gained conviction about the best direction to take the program in.

They were also about to get another bump, a second McCown boy at quarterback. And this time they were going to make sure they had the right plan in place.

Matt Turner, Luke Turner, Luke McCown, Randy McCown, Josh McCown, Jeff Traylor, and Jordan Traylor pose for a picture together. Traylor and Turner coached all three McCowns at quarterback and later coached both of their sons at the position. (Courtesy of Josh McCown)

An emotional Randy McCown is embraced by his parents, Pat and Robin, after defeating archrival Texas shortly after the Texas A&M Bonfire tragedy of 1999. (*The Eagle*/Butch Ireland)

"I don't need this. I'm single, I can go home, live with my momma, work at Wal-Mart. I've had enough of this."
--Kurt Traylor

Chapter 7: Little Brothers

When Randy McCown left Jacksonville for College Station in 1995, he anticipated a rerun of his glory days at Jacksonville. Instead, he found himself having to bide his time. As a redshirt freshman, he was used sparingly by Texas A&M's head coach, R.C. Slocum.

To add to his disappointment, McCown had arrived at Texas A&M during the aftermath of a tumultuous time. In 1990, the University of Arkansas had left the Southwest Conference (SWC) for the Southeastern Conference (SEC), and soon other SWC schools began holding private meetings with other conferences to discuss possible scenarios, the main two being the University of Texas (UT) and Texas A&M. Finally, in March of '94, the University of Texas, Texas A&M, Baylor University, and Texas Tech accepted invitations to join the more dominant Big 8 Conference. Together, they formed the Big 12.

In 1996, the same year that McCown began getting reps for the Aggies, the highly competitive Big 12 kicked off its first season. It was a tough transition for Texas A&M, and McCown witnessed the growing pains up close as the team went 6-6 and missed a bowl game for the first time ever during Slocum's tenure.

The next year proved equally disappointing when McCown was unexpectedly nudged aside by a blue-chip transfer, Branndon Stewart, during the first half of the season. McCown had had a poor start in a showdown with in-conference rival,

Texas Tech, so Slocum sent in Stewart, who almost pulled off a second-half comeback, which energized the team. That performance made Stewart the starting QB for the remainder of the season, and he rewarded his coach's confidence by leading the team to a Big 12 South title.

During high school, Stewart had been a prep All-American quarterback for Art Briles's Stephenville Yellow Jackets. Naturally, he was recruited by virtually every school in the country. He ended up choosing the University of Tennessee Volunteers because his style of play closely resembled that of the team's previous star quarterback, Heath Shuler. Unfortunately for Stewart, another All-American also chose to play for the Volunteers that season, a quarterback named Peyton Manning. Both Stewart and Manning shared playing time during their freshman season until week seven, when Coach Phillip Fulmer made the tough decision to build the team around Manning. Unwilling to play second fiddle, Stewart transferred to A&M, with a chance to finally lead a program.

But McCown was a tough competitor. Raised to hurdle even the highest obstacles, he did what McCowns do and put his nose to the grindstone, training himself mercilessly during the offseason. His work ethic impressed his coaches so much that Coach Slocum had no choice but to re-open the starting quarterback position.

The Aggies started the 1998 campaign with McCown and Stewart sharing duties. McCown was primed to turn up his wattage and secure a starting berth in week four's game against the University of North Texas. He completed 11-13 passes for two touchdowns and was back on top. With his gutsy playing, the Aggies picked up steam during their next five games, including a victory over number-two-ranked Nebraska.

But McCown's physical style of play could also be problematic. During the North Texas game, he suffered a separated shoulder, and this prevented him from starting in the next game, a Halloween-night matchup against Oklahoma. Stewart stepped in for McCown and brought the team to victory. Now A&M was one win away from capturing a Big 12 South title with only two remaining conference games left, and McCown thought his shoulder was healed enough for him to rejoin the team.

Two weeks later, on November 14, Texas A&M squeaked out a 17-14 victory over the number-13-ranked Missouri Tigers to capture the Big12 South title, and McCown reaffirmed Slocum's confidence in him. But there was still one game left, and this one had the highest stakes of all.

Texas A&M versus the University of Texas, the biggest game of the year for college football fans in Texas, was televised nationally either every Thanksgiving Day or the day after. Under a vibrant new head coach, Mack Brown, Texas was on the rise. True, it was still unranked, but the Longhorns had been competing against some of the powerhouses in the league, and even their losses showed a new level of skill and confidence. They also had the best player in college football that season, running back Ricky Williams.

After skyrocketing to a 23-7 lead on the wake of Williams, Texas looked set for a comfortable win. The offense was clicking, and Williams broke Tony Dorsett's NCAA record for yards in a season with his output of 244 yards that day. McCown was a fighter though, and the Aggies scratched and clawed their way back into the game.

Halfway into the fourth quarter, with the Aggies down 23-10, McCown delivered a touchdown strike to his tight end to make the game 23-17. After holding the Longhorns during the next series of plays, A&M began one final drive to win it. McCown led his team all the way down inside the Texas five-yard line and then on fourth and goal ran an option-keeper to the right and dove into the end zone for the go-ahead score. The drive was classic McCown. Texas A&M was now up 24-23, and it looked like they were going take down their rival.

But Longhorn freshman Major Applewhite wasn't yet finished. With under one minute to play, the young quarterback led Texas down the field with consecutive passes, setting up kicker Kris Stockton's game winning 24-yard field goal. A&M was devastated.

And McCown's day was about to get worse. At the end of the game, when he'd dived in for the go-ahead score, he'd broken his collarbone and was benched for the rest of the season, forced to watch Stewart lead the Aggies for its final two, and most important, games of the year.

Stewart performed well in the conference title game, defeating Kansas State for the program's first ever Big 12 championship, and the Aggies received a bid to play in the BCS Sugar Bowl, one of college football's most iconic bowl games. It was a charmed finish to a remarkable season for Stewart, and a sweet way to wind up his collegiate career. McCown would still have one more year, and little did he know that he would end up delivering the Aggies its most important win in school history.

In November of 1999, McCown aimed to cap off his career with a signature win against the arch-rival Longhorns. He had never beaten them as the starter, and this was going to be his final chance to play—and to behold the spectacle of the Aggie Bonfire, one of A&M's proudest traditions.

The bonfire is held annually on the eve of the Longhorns game, a tradition dating back to 1907. Its spectacular height launched it into the Guinness Book of World Records in 1969, when the towering stack of logs reached an unprecedented 109 feet, 10 inches.

But as students were preparing the logs in the early hours of November 18th, the stack collapsed, trapping several co-eds underneath and, ultimately, killing 12 students and injuring 27. The area's rescue operations took over for 24 hours nonstop and included members of the Corps of Cadets and the football team, all trying to find and free the trapped students.

The tragedy sparked national mourning. The two rival campuses came together as never before to grieve the deceased students, lend a hand of service, and prepare moving tributes. After careful consideration, Texas A&M officials decided to keep the game on as scheduled.

"I thought the players would be better, I thought our students would be better, and their families, to go ahead and play the game," said Aggie head coach R.C. Slocum in an interview with Bryan-College Station's *The Eagle*. "That we could draw some comfort from each other being together, rather than letting the kids go ahead and everybody leave for the holidays and be scattered everywhere."

The University of Texas entered the game ranked number seven in the country and was the early favorite. But *this* game was different. The bonfire tragedy was indelibly etched in the memories of the team and inspired them to outperform themselves.

With Texas leading 16-13 and driving late in the fourth quarter, A&M was in trouble. It needed a big play and got one with a forced fumble. Randy McCown was ready for his signature moment.

After driving all the way down to the Texas 14-yard line, McCown delivered a perfect fade pass into the end zone to put the Aggies up 20-16. This time, when Texas and Applewhite got the ball, A&M's defense would do anything to foil another dramatic Longhorns comeback.

After dropping back to pass, Applewhite was hit from another Aggie defender, and the ball was loose. Brian Gamble recovered it securely for the win. With it clear to all in attendance that the game was going to be a win for A&M, Gamble raised his face and lifted his hands to the sky in a tribute to the bonfire victims. It was a glorious ending for the season—and the perfect finale to McCown's career as an Aggie.

"You can't put it into words," McCown said in his postgame press conference. "A game like this is something you wish for all your life."

***

As one of the most celebrated Aggies of all time, McCown had set the bar stratospherically high for his two younger brothers, Josh and Luke. Josh was next up to play for the Indians, but he would have to be patient because he was a late bloomer and was overshadowed by an outstanding 5'9, 160-pound quarterback, chosen by Danny Long as the QB starter.

The backup assignment devastated Josh.

"He wanted to quit his junior year, and go to the gym," added Traylor. "He still teases me that if I hadn't kept him from quitting, he'd be the next Steve Nash."

The McCowns were stung but understood Long's decision, not that they liked it. Robin McCown, the family matriarch who had passed her competitive spirit down to her sons, was especially upset.

Pat McCown confided to Traylor, "I'll be supportive, but you need to stay away from Robin."

The move had paid off. The Indians went three rounds deep into the playoffs and improved their record from 3-7 to 10-3. The fans crowding into the Tomato Bowl were ecstatic, as was the entire community.

"The Tomato Bowl filled with those screaming fans is a moment I'll never forget," said offensive coach Wayne Coleman.

Coleman was riding high after a victorious season with the Indians—a highly visible success that caught the eye of administrators across the state, and he got his first head coaching job at Beeville ISD in South Texas. In the spring of 1997, Coleman bid Jacksonville goodbye.

"Beeville was almost identical to Jacksonville in regard to size and community," said Coleman. "I ended up only taking one guy with me, a linebacker coach named Brad Norvell, so the staff was still largely intact."

His departure opened the door for Traylor to help direct the offense alongside the remaining coordinator, Matt Turner.

With Traylor now in a higher role, there was also a need for a new offensive line coach, and Jeff's younger brother, Kurt, stepped into that role. That hiring was a clear signal by Long that he trusted Jeff's judgement.

Kurt Traylor had graduated from Gilmer in 1989 and then played offensive line, first at Cisco Junior College, and next at Southwest Baptist University. Like his older brother, he wanted to be a football coach, although he was somewhat reluctant to go into education, the field both his parents worked in.

"I saw how hard my mom and dad worked," said Kurt Traylor. "It motivated me to become a lawyer or doctor, but I love sports. And there's nothing like impacting kids' lives. It's a calling—as Biblical as a job can be."

After completing his education degree, Traylor accepted a job at West Rusk Middle School in New London. After just a year, Jacksonville came calling. But, as Jeff undoubtedly warned his younger brother, being Danny Long's offensive line coach was no easy task. Long had cut his teeth as an offensive line coach; while he gave a great deal of autonomy to other position coaches, that was the one he clung to.

"I had to win him over," said Kurt Traylor. "I really did. Because I was a new-school guy. I was a give-up-ground type guy on steps. He wasn't. His approach was to hit them and hit them harder. Jeff used to tell me that I had inherited the hardest job at Jacksonville because I was working with a guy who knows offensive line. He'd tell me that I'd better have a backup plan every day."

Long was notorious for disappearing from a drill and then reappearing at the most unexpected times because he was always juggling multiple responsibilities. But on the field or not, he kept close watch over his coaches, lest they stray from his style.

"I was a big Milt Tenopir guy," said Kurt. "I studied his work at Nebraska, and I'd pitch his techniques to Danny."

The same dialogue always ensued.

Long would call Kurt's suggestion "bull crap," and Kurt would remonstrate, "Coach, he's the o-line coach for Nebraska! Just let me start incorporating some of his moves."

Long's inevitable reply: "All right. But if you mess it up, I'm going to fire your ass."

Long was still as ruthless as he'd been with Jeff, and Kurt—like his older brother—thought about quitting after a disastrous game.

"I remember we swung the gate, and the whole defense cut us. It was a train wreck. And I barely took it in before Long was on my ass, telling me my kids were soft," Kurt said.

Kurt stood up for his players, telling Long, "They cut us, man. I'll get it fixed."

The conversation escalated from there.

"Quit making excuses for them," Long answered back.

"I'm not making excuses. I'm just telling you!" Kurt said. "Then Long told me to 'shut the fuck up.'"

That was the last straw for Kurt, who responded, "I'll tell you what, my ass is gone at halftime!"

True to his word, he started, "packing my crap up. It's in the middle of the game, mind you."

In a way, Kurt held the trump card. He was single, and he could always go home to Gilmer, so he faced Long down: "I don't need this. I'm single, I can go home, live with my momma, work at Wal-Mart. I've had enough of this. My kids are busting their ass," he said.

For all his bluster, Long didn't want to lose Kurt—not mid-season. And, especially, not mid-game.

In a rare show of respect for an assistant coach, Long finally just said, "I got ya."

"It was a small thing, but he finally trusted me because I showed him I was busting my ass and that I had guts," Kurt said. "Then some of our kids started getting recruited by SMU and A&M, and he told me, 'All right, you little young punk. Do what you want to do. It's all yours.'"

Long later admitted, "Kurt is the only guy that I'd relinquish that position to."

With Wayne gone and Kurt on board, Turner and the elder Traylor were now in control of the offensive game, and their quarterback was none other than the next McCown brother, Josh. Impartially assessing him, both coaches saw his finesse with the ball and went all in on the passing game for the Indians' offense.

"We liked to spread the ball around, but Jeff took it to another level," said Long. "He and Matt Turner worked incredibly well together. Jeff is really global, and Matt is very specific and detailed. Jeff wanted Matt's granular knowledge. They balanced each other so well that they acted as one. I'd never had time for Matt's specific knowledge—it's way *too specific* for me."

The duo were information junkies, travelling all over the state, and sometimes even outside the state, to pick the minds of more experienced coaches like Gary Joseph at Katy and Gus Malzahn at Tulsa.

Traylor wanted to make the most of his new star quarterback. He was like a big brother to Josh, calling him a "kindred spirit." The chemistry they had was evident. Jacksonville finished the regular season with a perfect 10-0 record, the first time in 20 years they had achieved that feat.

With a previous winning season under his belt, Long also wanted to strengthen the defense, and Jeff recommended an old friend from Big Sandy named Todd Barr. It was the second chapter of a professional bond that would last the next 18 years.

A native of Tyler, Barr had worked with Traylor the first time when Barr had begun his coaching career at Big Sandy under Brad McGinnis.

"We were great friends," said Barr. "We both lived in Tyler and drove back and forth from the school together. He always had a passion for the game, wanted to get better, and you could tell that he was going to be a head coach. That was his North Star. It was only a matter of time."

Barr had remained at Big Sandy for only a year and a half before moving to Bullard, a rapidly growing school district located just outside of Tyler. There, he coached defensive tackles; and, after one more brief stint at Big Sandy, he joined Jeff at Jacksonville.

"It was a 4A school, and there was opportunity to grow," Barr said. "They were starting to be successful. I wanted to be on board with the Jacksonville coaches."

Barr's first year with the Indians was Josh McCown's last, and the expectations were high for both. The Indians thought it could be their year. Then that dream collided with the Stingarees of Texas City.

In the third round of the playoffs, boasting a perfect 12-0 record, Jacksonville took the field against Texas City, which had an 11-1 record. The Stingarees were loaded. Eight graduating players had signed letters of intent to play college football, including four players who elected to play together at the University of Texas.

"They were so much physically better than us," said Long. "I remember game-planning and drawing three circles on the board. I knew we'd have to get the ball to the hole in the middle of the field against cover two safeties; we've got to get the ball behind the 8-technique in the flat; and I don't think I can block them to hand the ball to Richard Whitaker."

"Jeff and Matt put together an unbelievable game plan that got the ball in those spots, and we blocked just enough and ran a few draws," Long said.

Traylor concurred that, "We probably didn't run the ball ten times that game and ended up losing on the last play."

The matchup was a personal best for Josh McCown, including one signature play that almost put the game out of reach for Texas City. On fourth and goal from the eighteen-yard line, McCown rolled left and delivered a strike to receiver Adam Jimenez on the left goal line hash for the go-ahead touchdown.

"The Texas City head coach said it was the best throw he's ever seen," said Long. "It was a frozen rope."

With a little over a minute left, Texas City took the field down 27-28 and marched 70 yards down to the Jacksonville two-yard line. They decided to run a quarterback sneak to win on a touchdown, and the quarterback fumbled.

"It took thirty seconds to get everyone sorted out in the pile," said Long. "You could've heard a pin drop."

Texas City recovered its fumble, and then kicker Jody Kleinhans delivered a 19-yard field goal with one second on the clock for the 30-28 win.

"Josh played as good as any high school quarterback I've ever seen," said Traylor. "It was also the greatest game I've ever seen Danny coach. He was a pleasure to be around. He was totally at peace about the loss. He was awesome that night."

Texas City went on to win its next two games convincingly and captured the 1997 4A state championship. Josh was rewarded for his outstanding play by being named District 17-4A Offensive Player of the Year and the East Texas Player of the Year. Not bad for a kid who didn't start until he was a senior.

But Josh wasn't heavily recruited, to the surprise of his coaches and his family.

"Back then, a lot of schools didn't really have people on their radar unless they'd had a standout junior or sophomore year. This was before everyone had Hudl accounts and you had to rely on word of mouth and old videos," said Pat. "Baylor and SMU recruited him, and he eventually chose SMU. Unfortunately, he was forced to play early as a freshman on a bad team. He played three years there and got the crap beaten out of him."

McCown started 25 games for the Mustangs in three years; but after three consecutive losing seasons, he decided to transfer to Division I-AA Sam Houston State, the Bearkats.

"That was a multi-million-dollar decision right there," said Pat McCown. "He regained his love for the game and ended up leading the team to a conference championship and then all the way to the semifinals against Montana."

Long and Turner flew with the McCowns to see Josh play in the semifinals in Missoula, in eight-degree weather.

"There was a 30-mile per hour wind," said McCown. "I remember me and Danny were in the hotel having coffee, and here comes Matt walking like a stiff-legged dog after being on a two to three mile walk in shorts and a t-shirt. I told him he was crazy."

Turner replied, "This will get your blood going!"

The Bearkat offense had been a perfect fit for McCown, who ended up throwing for more touchdowns in his one season at Sam Houston than he did in all three years at SMU combined. For his efforts, he was named a third team All-American as well as the Southland Conference Player of the Year.

He also was about to have an opportunity to do something that Randy never did. In the third round of the 2002 NFL draft, the Arizona Cardinals selected Josh McCown with the 81st overall pick.

With two accomplished quarterbacks in one family, it was time for the third McCown brother to make his mark.

***

"Luke McCown was very self-confident," said Matt Turner. "He just didn't see obstacles, so the only limits he had were ours. And what we didn't know."

Jeff Traylor found Luke the most talented of the McCown brothers.

"He was freakish. He could go to the gym right now and do the Dominique Wilkins windmill dunk," Traylor said. "And you talk about cocky! To this day, Luke still thinks he's better than Drew Brees. He's got some swag to him. He acted like he always shot the biggest buck and caught the biggest fish—and, to be honest, he probably did."

The Indians went 8-4 both seasons with Luke at the helm but never advanced past the Area round. It was an offensive show to watch though, and Luke was the star.

"He was probably the number one or number two recruit in the country," said Pat. "Luke had more letters than I could keep in my house."

Danny Long implored Pat to take Luke to Florida State University and at least get a gander at the Seminoles, but Pat stood firm. He didn't want his son to go to a school outside a three-hour driving radius of Jacksonville.

"We weren't poor, but we couldn't afford to fly all over the country to see his games—even though we wound up doing just that," McCown said.

Somewhat exasperated, Long told him, "Well, how about *you* be the one to tell Bobby Bowden that he's not going to FSU then."

"I had a good laugh about that one," said Pat.

Luke eventually chose Louisiana Tech, which, just as his father had wished, kept him close to home. He was arguably the highest-ranking recruit ever to commit to the Bulldogs; and by week five of his freshman season, head coach, Jack Bicknell, declared that the Luke McCown era had begun.

That year, McCown set three NCAA passing records that still hold up today; and, as a sophomore, he led the Bulldogs to the Western Athletic Conference (WAC) championship, its first conference championship in 17 years. During his college career, he started 44 straight games and became one of the best players in Louisiana Tech history.

In the fourth round of the 2004 NFL draft, yet another McCown boy was selected to join the pros. The Cleveland Browns chose Luke with the 106th overall pick.

"In the Browns facility, there were these big air-ducts about 12.5 feet above your head," said Pat. "One of those guys in the hallways asked Luke if he could jump up and touch it. Well, Luke has never lacked confidence, so he jumped up and touched it. Within five minutes, all these people were placing bets to see if he could do it again. I'm talking thousands of dollars in bets. I couldn't make that up."

"Even when he eventually got traded to Tampa Bay, Jon Gruden used to keep a tape of when Luke did the Vince Carter between his legs to win a dunk contest. He used to show it to everyone who came into the Tampa Bay organization."

The McCown family was indeed one of a kind. They had blessed Jacksonville in more ways than it ever could have imagined.

There was mutual love between the McCowns and the Jacksonville staff, especially for quarterback coach Matt Turner.

"Matt is the best coach and teacher I've ever been around at any level," said Pat. "His influence on my boys—the attention to detail. They still have it to this day."

The McCowns had become part of the Indians' identity, a facet of the rare culture created by Danny Long.

"You have to remember Danny took over a program that was nothing," said Kurt Traylor. "At the core of that culture was an emphasis on relationships. That and accountability."

Long even created a Coach's Mission Statement based on Colossians 3:23: "Life's mission is to be true to God, true to family and then work at your job as if you were working for the Lord and not for men."

"That's literally how we tried to live," said Kurt.

Long's mission statement would eventually show up in several programs that were birthed out of that Jacksonville coaching staff—and the time was coming for Jacksonville to beget a lot of head coaches.

"I really believe if Danny could've kept our staff together, we would've won a state championship," said Kurt. "We came so close."

Wayne Coleman had been the first of the core members to go out on his own, and that started the elder Traylor thinking about his future.

"I remember after a few years had gone by, Jeff tells me that he's not sure he wants to leave and be a head coach," said Coleman. "And Jeff is a very spiritual guy. I told him, 'Do you think God's plan is for Wayne, Danny, Jeff, and Matt never to leave and grow other communities?' It's just tough because everyone was always so focused on their purpose, and you can get caught up in winning rather than living your own life."

Danny Long was also hugely helpful to Jeff as he mulled over his future and his ambition to be a head coach.

"I remember in 1998, right after we had the great year with Josh, Danny called me into his office," said Traylor. "I'm still driving my 1985 Camaro T-top, and he tells me, 'You know you're going to be considered for a head coaching job really soon, and they're not going to hire someone who drives a Camaro. You need to go sell it and buy a truck.' I told him that I couldn't afford a truck, so he told me to go to Mr. McCray at the Ford dealership, and he would give me a good deal. Sure enough, two years after I got my truck, I got my head coaching job."

The path to that job was very different and far more humbling than Jeff had ever imagined.

After the 1999 season, Aubrey ISD, which is just north of the Metroplex, offered Jeff its head job.

"I didn't feel good about it, so I pulled out of that one," Traylor recalled.

Next, came Edna, a 4A community in South Texas.

"The superintendent was fantastic. Their administration even came up to Jacksonville to visit and stay the night. They offered, and I was going to take it. Then Danny called me."

Long let Traylor know that the school board had worked out a scenario so that Jeff could be promoted to the top job, and Long would transition into a role as the district's athletic director. So, Traylor turned Edna down.

A week later, Long broke the news that the board changed its mind and wanted to wait one more year before starting the transition.

"I was crushed. I had just let the Edna job go. I had a mid-life crisis at age thirty," Traylor said.

Picking himself up, Traylor interviewed for other jobs. His old mentor, Wayne Coleman, had a word of advice: never take a job just for the sake of becoming a head coach.

"But I did tell him to keep his head on a swivel and keep his options open because at some point there would be a program that wanted him and that he could grow exactly as he saw fit," Coleman said.

Indeed, after just a few weeks, an ideal job landed in Traylor's lap.

"A good friend had told me the Gilmer job was opening up, and I told him that there was no way they'd ever hire me. I was too much of a hoodlum," he said.

"I still remember Greg Owens [former head coach of Sulphur Springs] telling me I was crazy because Gilmer was the worst job in the state. I still give him hell over that," said Traylor.

The young and idealistic coach refused to believe what others said about his hometown.

"The thing is my mother had been a teacher there, and she told me those kids were underachieving and that there was a lot of division between the White community and the Black community," said Traylor. "I was one of the few that had great rapport with both sides. I really felt like I could pull those two communities together."

In Traylor's view, "Everything is about timing and fit in this business. I was the perfect fit."

Knowing Jeff wanted it, Long quickly made a call to Gilmer's superintendent, Dr. Larry Bennett, explaining that if Bennett wanted to keep his job as superintendent, he had better hire Jeff Traylor.

"I'm pretty sure that pissed Bennett off," said Traylor. "But Bennet eventually told me, 'I'll give you an interview because your mother was the best teacher my daughter ever had.'"

The interview, scheduled for 30 minutes, lasted for three hours. Jeff was hired as head coach on a 4-3 vote by the Gilmer school board and awarded a probationary contract for $52,000.

Now Gilmer bound, Jeff Traylor had come full circle.

Keith Tate and Olan Johnson, both pictured in the center with their hands on their hips, helped lay the foundation for Gilmer football in 2000. Tate did it as a coach, while Johnson was the program's first quarterback when Traylor took over as head coach. In 2014, Johnson reunited with Tate and his other former coaches when he joined his alma mater as a coach. (Courtesy of Donya Denman)

In 2004 at Stephen F. Austin's Homer Bryce Stadium, Gilmer played the Jasper Bulldogs for the 3A state championship. (Courtesy of Cari Traylor)

"Love is the most powerful force on earth, and I think Jeff is the embodiment of a loving head coach."
--Danny Long

Chapter 8: PRIDE

In July 2000, Jeff Traylor arrived in Gilmer to a team that had had one winning season in the past five years and hadn't been to the playoffs in almost ten. Resources were low, and morale was even lower.

"At the time it was a very selfish, me-driven place. It was not a program. It was a bunch of individual sports, and we needed it to be about the Buckeyes," said Traylor.

Traylor immediately grasped that his challenge wasn't just to make a better team; it was to make a better school. The students were underachieving, and there was a prevailing feeling of inertia. Traylor knew that if his program was to succeed, he needed to hit the reset button on Gilmer and what it stood for.

"I wanted the Buckeyes to be proud of their team, their school, and their town," he said.

He started by creating a new Buckeye slogan, PRIDE—an acronym for Pride, Respect, Intensity, Discipline, Every Play. These were the qualities he valued in himself and the ones he wanted to instill in the boys on his team. "Every Play" meant that the players would work tirelessly for each point and every inch of ground, never lying down to their opponents.

Achieving excellence meant rejecting mediocrity. Traylor immediately started reshaping the coaching staff in his vision for the program. Out of the 18 coaches there when he arrived, he kept only two: Keith Tate, the young basketball coach who was a Gilmer native, and Max Low, the junior high coordinator. It wasn't experience he was looking for but intelligence and character. After making some initial changes, he began assembling a coaching staff second to none, men he trusted to dedicate themselves to Gilmer and bring out the best in every kid. He started by luring some talent away from Jacksonville head coach Danny Long, first going after the outstanding defensive coach Todd Barr.

"I still remember Jeff initially asking me to go, and I wasn't sure because it was so late in the year, with the beginning of the season a month away," said Barr. "Jeff told me to come over and meet the kids, so I did. I could just tell they were hungry and wanted direction. I was in from that moment forward."

In addition to Barr, Traylor convinced Phil Pate and Craig Barker to be on his staff.

"Our philosophies all lined up. Plus, we loved each other, and we wanted the chance to see what we could all achieve together," Barr said. "Gilmer has always had some good athletes, we had seen that on film, but we wanted to instill pride and discipline into the program."

Also on board were a group of young assistants, including Jeff's brother, Kurt, another Gilmer native, who had kept tabs on his alma mater, sometimes unhappily.

"I remember coaching in Jacksonville and going to scout Carthage when they were playing at Gilmer," said Kurt. "There's maybe a 100 people in the stands, and there's kids everywhere. And Gilmer played Carthage's butt off in the first half then laid down in the second half. They were always doing something stupid and getting their butt beat."

One of Traylor's first priorities was giving his team confidence from the outside in by fixing the rundown fieldhouse, the embodiment of the apathy Jeff had found at Gilmer. He enlisted Kurt to help him.

"I came in and put carpet down, the cheapest I could find," said Jeff. "I painted whatever I could paint. Next, I worked on their gym clothes and got them new t-shirts and shorts that matched. I washed their clothes every day and hung them in their lockers. Ultimately, I was trying to change a culture of excuse-making, finger-pointing, and apathy."

Apathy had become so baked into the Gilmer culture that Jeff's home improvements befuddled the rest of the school. Why bother to make all the changes? But he persisted. The next phase of Traylor's mission was the most important for success. He reinvented the rules about how the football team accepted players. The old coaches had either kicked out or driven away many of the kids, so he let every boy who wanted to come back into the program, no matter their reputation.

"I just treated it as all sins are forgiven," he said.

In addition, Jeff and the other coaches started spending as much time with the players as they could—one of his mandates for his staff. To his astonishment, he learned that these kids had never practiced after school, just during their gym period, so it was a rude awakening when practice became a requirement for playing.

"Some of them thought I was a pretty mean person for having an actual practice," he said. "I wasn't received really well by everyone, and a lot of them eventually quit. But the really good kids, I attracted a lot of them back. It was kind of like a transformation. All the knuckleheads left, so we had a core of kids I enjoyed being around. They embraced the change."

Traylor's family, too, had to adjust to change. Now that he was a head coach, he was putting in even more grueling hours than he had in Jacksonville.

"I remember moving into a new house in Gilmer," said Cari, "and it was the biggest house we'd ever lived in. And we're laying in bed late at night, the house is quiet, and he couldn't sleep. The wheels were constantly turning in his head, and I remember him saying, 'I'm going to be working a lot more, a whole lot more.'"

Traylor outlined two initial objectives for his staff: get the high school team ready for the opening game against archrival, Gladewater, and build the junior high program.

"I literally had one month to get ready for Gladewater," he said. "And I worked the kids hard because I knew that if we won that game, I'd have a lifetime contract. Sure enough, we did it."

The player who contributed the most to the Gladewater game was quarterback Olan Johnson. At 6'3, 200 pounds, Johnson was smart, fast, and, most important in Jeff's eyes, high-minded with a quick intellect and a ton of character.

"He was pretty much my whole team. He brought in value from day one," Traylor said. "We had so many kids quit early. We only had about twenty-five or thirty on varsity, eighteen on the ninth-grade squad, and fifteen on the JV. I wanted so badly to have a schedule for all three teams, and I did my best. Our JV ended up going zero for ten, but we made it through the entire season even though we got killed every Thursday. Our ninth grade was about .500."

The good news was that there was talent downstream in the junior high school. Jeff's staff spent a lot of time there getting to know the kids, so soon there were 60 kids on the seventh grade, and 55 on the eighth-grade team. True to form, the staff was down on the field for both the junior high and 9th & JV games on Thursday nights, the precious hours when Traylor felt "the pure joy of coaching."

The varsity battled through a tough stretch. The previous two seasons had seen the Buckeyes go 5-5. It was important to the overall psyche of the program to gain some tangible improvement, and Homecoming was the game that got them over the mark.

"We were down 13-7 with a little over a minute left in the game," recalled Johnson. "I remember on the previous play I threw a perfect ball to one of our receivers that would've sealed the game, but it just went out of his hands. So, on fourth down, Coach Traylor called timeout, and then he called a variation of the exact same play. When we ran it this time, the corner bit, and our receiver Larry Reeves beat his man downfield. I rolled out and heaved it up. Larry scored and we won the game."

Gilmer finished 6-4 in Traylor's debut season. It was a winning record, the first in years, but the Buckeyes still came in third, just missing the playoffs.

"We weren't ready to go the distance," said Traylor. "We were closer. We had a winning season, and we did beat Gladewater, but we got blasted by Spring Hill and Daingerfield. We didn't know how to compete yet."

The better news was that both of the junior high groups went undefeated. Even though the season didn't fully meet Traylor's expectations, there was momentum in the program for the first time in years.

"We had a little moxie about us down on the field, and the buzz kind of got out," Traylor said.

"I did brash things that I probably wouldn't do again. I predicted a state championship. I said we were going to kill everybody, and we were going to kick the other teams' butts. I stirred up a mess, you know. Everybody was talking about us. I'm sure they were laughing at us, but I didn't care. I wanted our kids to have a little swagger about themselves."

The staff was taking ownership of Traylor's vision, and coaches found creative ways to give their players the mindset of fearsome competitors.

One night Barr was reading a *Nike Coach of the Year* clinic book, and it featured a Division II team that put an opponent's mascot on a black flag every time they beat them and then flew the flag at practice.

"I stole the idea. We told the kids that in wartime, you communicated with flags and each color had a different significance," he said. "A white flag meant you surrendered. A yellow flag meant you needed medical supplies, and a black flag meant you were going to fight to the death and hold your ground no matter what the odds were."

The Buckeyes started calling their defense "The Black Flag."

"It just kind of started that way and then it grew and grew. I never thought it would be as popular as it became," Barr said.

Traylor kept a close eye on his coaching staff. One season wasn't going to transform the program's DNA, and he wasn't afraid to fire coaches who didn't buy into a new culture of pride and achievement.

"It was just mind-boggling to me how inconsistent the team could be," Jeff said. "In the past, they'd occasionally beat a Kilgore and then lose to a White Oak or a Spring Hill. Not that those are bad schools, but they don't have near the talent that Gilmer does. I wanted to make sure we didn't slip backwards."

To keep the staff sharp, he let some coaches go and he brought on new blood. One of Traylor's biggest staff gets after his initial season was offensive coordinator Alan Metzel, who'd coached at Union Grove under Mike Maddox.

"That was a really special time working with Maddox," said Metzel. "It was never my goal to go to Union Grove, but I met him, and he was just a dynamic man that could get blood out of a turnip. Mike is an unbelievable motivator."

Alan switched to Gilmer, in part, because he and his wife, Jana, had adopted two children, and his Union Grove salary wasn't paying the bills.

"We were struggling. Jeff offered a quarterback coach position. I knew they had ability there, and he also offered me the head girls basketball and girls coordinator positions," Metzel said. "That was a ten thousand dollar raise for us, which was a big deal to our family. The funny thing is I ended up talking Maddox into joining us the following year."

Traylor proved quite adept not only at attracting top coaches but also at getting the community—most importantly, the local power brokers—to adopt the team.

"I had a lot of help from behind the scenes getting the resources I needed," said Traylor. "James Beall, who had been my high school coach, was a big supporter; so was Henry Jackson, my junior high coach, and James Heffernan who was on the school board at the time and who had actually coached me too. Another board member, Elliott Dean, was also in my corner. They all lobbied for us to get the resources we needed."

"We even had guys like Matt Camp, and Rebel Jackson," added Metzel. "People like that would help our 7-on-7 team, help with school supplies, and even help guys get lawn mower and roofing jobs for the kids and the coaches to make extra money. Steve York came on as our trainer. He used to be the trainer for Jimmy Johnson and Eddie Sutton at Oklahoma State. He'd just moved to Gilmer to raise his family, and he's one of those guys who sets the standard for work ethic. There is no job beneath him, and he'll do anything to help."

The staff also reached out to the community to serve in the Adopt-a-Buckeye program, which made sure every player on the team had someone to meet them down on the field once the game was over.

"Adopt-a-Buckeye was huge," said Traylor. "We then started Meet the Buckeyes, which was a big community pep rally to kick off the season. We just kept getting our community increasingly involved, including the teachers."

It still wasn't all smooth sailing, though. At the start of the 2001 season, projected quarterback Jamal Gaines moved to the Metroplex at the last minute with his mother. The next best option was to go with the most talented freshman on the team, Manuel Johnson, but then his grandmother moved him out to Garland.

"So, we ended up playing Clint Quinn, which was a lucky thing," said Traylor. "Clint was a senior and the valedictorian, the greatest kid ever. And Clint won a district championship for us."

The championship had been clinched when Buckeye Don Griffin scooped and scored on a Tatum Eagle fumble deep in Gilmer's territory. Then, in the first round of the playoffs, the Buckeyes went on to lose to Pleasant Grove by a score of 10-0. That was the last time that Gilmer was ever shut out under Traylor.

The discipline and focus he brought to athletics extended to academics.

"We did tutorials every Tuesday after school," said Traylor. "We didn't start football practice until after six o'clock at night. We never lost a kid to grades at Gilmer, not one kid on varsity. We had all of the coaches in the halls and at four o'clock all of our kids were in tutorials for an hour or until they were done. We wanted every teacher to know we had their backs. We basically became free assistant principals."

***

He'd learned how to build a program under Danny Long's wing, and that included getting students to embrace leadership.

"We started doing Captain's Council on Monday nights," said Traylor. "Our coaches and players voted, and I'd meet with anywhere from eight to twelve seniors, and we'd just have dinner together and do a leadership study. Some of my best memories are being with those kids after a long practice and just listening to them talk."

Traylor and his staff were big on message repetition. Each week, the team would hear about a designated character trait, such as dedication, and it would be talked about from two assistant coaches, a pastor, and Traylor himself, all leading up to Friday's game.

"Those self-led teams are hard to beat," said Traylor. "You've got to turn them loose eventually, so you better have guys out there spreading your message. The only way they're going to know your message is if you teach it to them. I think things like Captain's Council and all the talks we had about character are everything, and I will always believe that."

He lived by his coaching mission statement, a Bible passage from Colossians 3:23. "Life's mission is to be true to God, true to your family, and then to work at your job as you were working for the Lord and not for men."

There was another key factor that was critical to Traylor realizing his vision, the full-fledged support of the new superintendent.

"Rick Albritton was as important to the success of Gilmer as anybody," said Traylor.

Albritton came to the district after Larry Bennett, who'd initially hired Traylor, retired after the 2001 school year. Albritton had been the assistant superintendent for Longview High School, where he'd overseen financial services.

"Most first-time superintendents are going to have to start at the 2A level, but because of Gilmer's financial troubles at the time and my background in finance, I met the bill," said Albritton.

He came in with a clear understanding of what he was facing.

"My initial priorities were to have a written curriculum that was deep and accessible to all teachers, to get our facilities updated because some of the buildings were in shameful condition, and then to bring up the morale of students and teachers at the school. They had gone through a difficult time the previous three years when they'd tried to pass a bond and it failed."

Albritton was immediately drawn to the mission of Traylor and his staff.

"Jeff was all about building pride in that program and building character in the kids. Treating people with respect. When a play was over, they picked up the ball and took it to the referees. Our kids picked up other kids off the ground. Jeff gave us a strong foundation to spread to the rest of the school," he said.

"Mr. Albritton was a godsend coming from Longview," added Jeff. "He had come from a culture where football was very important, and he understood the importance of it in East Texas. He really took care of me and my coaches."

Metzel recalled Albritton telling him, "If there is an issue you have, come and tell me. I'll try and get it fixed."

The 2002 season was a woeful reminder of the previous year. Again, the Buckeyes claimed the district title but got knocked out of the playoffs in the first round.

"We lost a heartbreaker to Daingerfield in the playoffs," said Traylor. "We had outplayed them. We blocked their field goal, and they picked it up and ran it for a touchdown. Then, we ran a Quarterback Power, on the one-yard line, and they knocked it out of our hands and went 99 yards for a touchdown. We just weren't ready to beat Daingerfield yet, but we had outplayed them."

One silver lining emerged from that game.

"Matt Turner came to watch the Daingerfield game. Once it was over, he came down on the field, walked over to me, and said simply, 'I'm ready to join,'" said Traylor.

Turner had initially turned down the invitation to join Traylor's staff when Jeff first got the job, but after his boss, Danny Long, had been offered a job in Baytown following Jacksonville's fifth district title, the opportunity to join was finally too enticing to turn down. Turner could have joined Long in Baytown, but he knew that Jeff was turning Gilmer into a great program, and he wanted to be a part of that energy. East Texas had also become his family's home.

Traylor made Turner a co-offensive coordinator with Alan Metzel. While some coaches might have been threatened by sharing a title, Metzel and Turner embraced working together. They were too similar not to get along.

"Both of them are servants, so they don't get into petty stuff," said Traylor.

Their new partnership became an extraordinary advantage for the Buckeye offense.

"Coach Turner and Coach Metzel working together in unison was a thing of beauty," said Keith Tate. "I'd watch how Coach Traylor would give them some broad aspects of an offensive scheme, and then they would figure out all of the minutiae that went with it."

The level of detail that they brought to the offensive plans was Turner's strong suit. Traylor now had a core group of football coaches—Alan Metzel, Kurt Traylor, Matt Turner, and Todd Barr—that he could put up against anyone.

"Jeff's ability to get coaches to come to Gilmer was an amazing asset to the program, and it took a lot of work," said Metzel. "It wasn't easy to coach here at that time. Sometimes when kids didn't show up for practice, we'd actually drive out to their homes to pick them up and bring them back to school. We even corralled a kid who was hiding behind the curtains in his living room. It's remarkable how much effort we put into this job."

The 2003 season proved to be the breakthrough. The Buckeyes finished the regular season with a perfect 10-0 record. Then, they got their revenge on number-one-ranked Daingerfield in the first round of the playoffs and followed that up by beating perennial powers Celina and Tatum.

"To me, that was when we really got it going," said Todd Barr. "The 2002 and 2003 offseason training camps were pivotal, and in 2003 we went all the way to the top four in the playoffs, but we lost to Atlanta, and they went on to win state. We had a great team, but we just ran out of gas."

After achieving its most promising season in over two decades, Gilmer had no intention of looking back, even though the Buckeyes lost twenty starters to graduation. Traylor was especially looking forward to the 2004 season, which would bear the fruits of the junior varsity initiatives he'd started back in his first year. The eighth-grade class he'd coached had moved up to the varsity team and it was time to deliver. That season, too, the senior class had a star player who Traylor believed could get them over the hump.

Manuel Johnson had been the best athlete in his Gilmer eighth-grade class, initially playing quarterback. After the start of high school, he'd moved to Garland and then returned to Gilmer as a star wide receiver for the next season, when he became the first player in program history to earn first team All-State honors for that position; but at the start of his senior year, his coaches needed him to switch back to being a quarterback again. Johnson was quiet, friendly, and unassuming, but he was also ferociously competitive.

"Manny is like a ninja," said former Longview Lobo Malcolm Kelly. "He's the nicest guy you'd ever want to meet as long as you're not lined up across from him. Then he turns into a killer."

Johnson had one of the most memorable high school careers in East Texas football history. He threw 48 touchdowns, ran for 18, and caught an additional 16. He easily set the school touchdown record; and his leadership, coupled with the young talent of future NFL players like Curtis Brown and David Snow, allowed Gilmer to coast to a 15-0 record with an opportunity to play for their first state title.

"It may sound kind of corny, but it goes back to what we learned in junior high when we went through the Buckeye Maker boot camp," said Johnson in an interview with *The Gilmer Mirror*. "Whether it's football, or college, or life in general, it's really all about being positive, respectful, intense, and disciplined in everything you do. Buckeye PRIDE—I bought into it in the eighth grade, and it's worked for me ever since."

Johnson and his teammates had changed the program for the better.

"Building a program is a mindset," said Turner. "The players, the community, the administration—you're trying to get people to be their very best, and it seems like it's a simple thing, but it's complicated to build a new culture. It's risky, and it takes time. The biggest thing is time. You've got to break old habits and old ways of thinking. It takes really good people committed to that, as well as talent. You've got to have both—and Gilmer always had that. God expects our best, and it's our mission to give that."

Late in 2004, Gilmer was set to play Jasper in the 3A state championship game in Homer Bryce stadium on the campus of SFA in Nacogdoches, a perfect setting for an East Texas state championship game.

"I still remember seeing our crowd at SFA when we arrived to play for the title," said Barr. "We had a couple hundred fans out there tailgating hours before the game."

The enthusiasm and belief in what they could do showed in the program's increased participation numbers. They finally had the bench to last deep into the playoffs.

"I think the number one indicator of quality high school football is depth," said Danny Long. "Kids are going to get hurt, fail classes, and get in trouble, so you have to factor in those things. It's the coaches' fault if they don't have a plan to deal with that."

The Buckeyes *had* a plan, and they executed it early against the Bulldogs of Jasper. Led by Johnson, who had already had a record-setting year, Gilmer held a three-touchdown lead for most of the game behind his ability to make plays. Adversity struck at the end though, and the contest ended up going down to the wire.

"We were up forty-two to twenty-one, and then Manny threw three interceptions on three consecutive drives. They scored every time and almost tied it up. They went for two and didn't get it, so it was forty-two to forty-one late in the fourth," said Traylor.

Clinging to a one-point lead, Johnson demonstrated why he was the eventual 3A Player of the Year. With 6:41 left in the game, Manny tossed a 61-yard strike to wide receiver Tay Bowser that gave them a 49-41 lead. Jasper would get another late score in, but it was too late for them to get the second one that they needed. Gilmer claimed its first state title in program history by a score of 49-47.

"It was special, man. Add in that the game was at SFA, where my wife and I went to college. It was really cool. The place was absolutely packed out, too," said Traylor.

It was also a family affair for the Traylor family; as Jeff's son, Jordan, was old enough to be a ball boy at the game.

"That was the first big moment for all of us—the biggest since we'd been at Gilmer," said Cari.

Metzel credited Traylor with having the vision to see Gilmer's potential.

"As soon as we got here, he began saying that we were going to win a state championship," Metzel said. "I guess those eighth graders sure did believe it."

Traylor gave kudos to Manuel Johnson's cohort.

"The fifty-five junior high kids, Manuel Johnson's group, were the ones who won that first state championship," said Traylor. "How about that? I even told them when I first took over that we'd win it in five years. And really, I was just praying that they would let me stay five. But that's exactly what we did, which was crazy."

Traylor's old Jacksonville mentor, Danny Long, couldn't have been prouder.

"I think Jeff took in what I learned from James Cameron and the booster club," said Danny Long, "And he absorbed what I learned from Dennis Parker and D.W. Rutledge when they were at Judson. Then he made it all his own."

"Jeff was so great about finding a better way of doing things though. He's a good human being. The basis of his life is he truly loves kids. And kids perform better and at a higher level when they're playing for something much bigger than a trophy; especially, when they love the guys they're playing next to and the coach they're playing for."

Danny Long summed it up, "Love is the most powerful force on earth, and I think Jeff is the embodiment of a loving head coach."

As head coach for the Lake Travis Cavaliers, Chad Morris captured back-to-back state championships in 2008 and 2009. During this time, Lake Travis became the premier high school program in the state. Morris is a native East Texan and close friend of Gilmer's Jeff Traylor. (*Austin American-Statesman*)

"Coach Traylor didn't care about Texas Tech. This was *his* program and this was the way they were going to do things. You're a part of the team, you're not bigger than the team."
--Blake Lynch

Chapter 9: The Passing Game

Gilmer was far from the only program in East Texas that was meeting success in the 2010s. The region boasted six state champions from 2010 to 2013. In a region where the football team's achievements were overshadowing any school's TEA academic rating, several superintendents quickly realized that an easy way to rally community support was to hire a hotshot football coach. While some schools plucked rising stars from local powers, others started pursuing athletic staff two or three notches below head coach from programs in the 5A and 6A blue bloods of the Dallas Metroplex and Houston areas—schools like Allen, Cedar Hill, and Katy—and offered them head coaching jobs.

In 2010, Longview's Spring Hill High School was the first to make the bold move when it chose to look outside of the Piney Woods and hire Bill Poe, a star offensive coordinator from the Dallas area's Southlake Carroll High School. The following year, rival high school White Oak made a similar move when it hired L.D. Bell High School's Gerry Stanford, yet another young offensive coordinator from the Metroplex. The similarities in both hires reflected more than just an admiration for larger districts. It reflected a change in philosophy. The new coaches were young, pass-oriented, and believed in playing fast, a basketball-on-turf approach that differed distinctly from the grind-it-out style that had epitomized teams in East Texas. In this gritty and hardworking region, blocking a team and then running it over at full bore, had been a strategy that mirrored the soul of the populace.

In 2000, a young Mike Leach came to Texas as head coach of Texas Tech's Red Raiders. His brand of offense was crafted out of his working relationship with Hal Mumme, inventor of the "Air Raid" offense, essentially, attacking the defense by spreading it out and going with a more aggressive, pass-oriented approach. It was a strategy devised of need. Texas Tech couldn't recruit the same level of athletes that played for the Big 12's blue bloods, so they gained an edge by doing something that no one else prepared for. The strategy paid off. In 2008, Mike Leach led his Red Raiders to an 11-2 record and a share of the Big 12 South title. For his efforts, he was named Big 12 Coach of the Year. He had proven that his brand of offense could bring a team with lesser talent to the highest levels.

Other Texas college coaches implemented similar systems with success. Former legendary Stephenville High School football coach, Art Briles, did the same thing at perennial doormat Baylor University when he led the Bears to Big 12 titles in 2013 and 2014; and Kevin Sumlin had just re-energized a Texas A&M fan base with an offense that produced a Heisman trophy recipient and an 11-win debut. Leach, Briles, and Sumlin demonstrated clearly that throwing the ball could be the great equalizer when you're lacking in size and strength. High school coaches across the state took notice and implemented similar strategies.

No program did a better job at throwing the ball than the Austin area's Lake Travis High School. Its mediocre program had been on the upswing since Coach Jeff Dicus took over the Cavaliers in 2003. Dicus came from South Texas's Mission High School, where he had turned its program around in only two years. Lake Travis had presented a new challenge, one that Dicus met readily. He understood that resources were paramount for a successful high school athletic program, and increased resources boiled down to increased budgets. He entered Lake Travis as it was transforming from a sleepy town to a burgeoning bedroom community for Austin, one of the fastest growing cities in the country at that time. Doctors and lawyers were moving in droves into a region once dominated by farmers and mill workers. With that influx of white-collar workers came a flood of money for sports programs.

A bigger budget enabled Discus to get the facilities and staff he needed to lead the Cavaliers to their first state championship in program history just five years after his arrival. He did it through the air, too, with a junior quarterback, Garrett Gilbert, who set state records for completions, pass attempts, and yards in a single season—and was rated number one in the country by the end of his junior year. Success built upon success as star quarterbacks from other districts started enrolling in the school to join the most dominant program from the two largest classifications during the decade between 2005-2014.

Change was expectedly fast, too, in the Cavaliers' leadership staff. Despite having Garrett Gilbert returning for his senior year, and a veteran team that was poised to compete for another championship, Dicus parlayed his success into what he thought was a better job in the Metroplex's Duncanville High School. Lake Travis was now a coveted position, and the leadership wanted another state championship-level coach who could handle the community's newfound expectations. They also wanted someone who knew how to win with a passing game. After careful consideration, they decided on Stephenville High School's Chad Morris.

Morris was a native of Edgewood, a small town in East Texas. He had already been a head coach at four different schools when he joined Lake Travis. While he had won at every place, including a state championship at Bay City, it was his tenure at Stephenville that best prepared him to unite and propel a growing community like Lake Travis.

"When I got to Stephenville and started coaching the Yellow Jackets, I had basically followed Art Briles," said Morris. "So, there were things set in stone that I couldn't change at first because that's the way Briles had done them at Stephenville."

"I turned away from what had made me successful at other schools. I was trying to be Art Briles, and I lost my swag, so to speak."

Morris had learned a valuable lesson. Cramping his style to fit that of another coach didn't bring results; it tanked them. Eventually, he established his own culture at Stephenville.

"It was after some hard rock times that I finally was able to get away with it," he said.

After an underwhelming first year, Morris went on to win at least ten games a season during his next four years at the helm. His best season came in 2005, when the Yellow Jackets, led by Parade All-American and University of Texas commit Jevan Snead, came up just three points short in the 4A semifinals to Highland Park and their All-American quarterback, Matthew Stafford. The game was dubbed one of the 10 most memorable by the popular online publication, *Max Preps*, American's leading source for high school sports news.

During this time, Chad Morris's good friend, Jeff Traylor, was busy trying to turn his alma mater, Gilmer, into a Stephenville. The two became close and shared ideas they were picking up from other schools and coaches.

"We were climbing up the ranks around the same time," said Traylor. "When he was at Eustace, I was at Big Sandy. And when he was at Elysian Fields and Bay City, I was at Jacksonville."

"Chad was so great for me. He would always give me advice on how to structure my teaching fields for my assistants, what salary to ask for, and the best way to organize the junior high program. He would just talk me through a lot of things."

Both men also had a deep loyalty to the fraternity of the Texas High School Coaches Association and to their region.

"We're both East Texas guys," said Traylor. "He's from Edgewood, and I'm from Gilmer. There's a shared outlook there."

***

When Morris moved to Austin to take over the Cavaliers, he was well prepared for success. He knew how to establish his version of a winning culture. He had an All-American quarterback, an administration that was ready to invest big-time in its facilities, and a vibrant community that wanted to be out of rival Austin Westlake's shadow. It was time to capitalize.

"The school and community turned out for games—and they loved it," said Morris. "They were relishing success. There was tailgating before games, and we'd have the Cavalier Walk. It was a big deal."

During his first year he surpassed expectations and beat Westlake.

"Westlake had had so much success and the communities are very close in distance and are very similar. The people in Lake Travis were hungry for a win over Westlake. So, that first year when we beat them, you really saw a community come together."

The Cavaliers more than beat Westlake. They didn't lose a game for two consecutive seasons, from 2008 to 2009, and both seasons culminated with Lake Travis beating East Texas powerhouse Longview High School in the 4A state championship game. The Cavaliers boasted the number-one ranked offense in Texas, and Morris was celebrated as the state's premier high school coach.

It didn't take long for colleges to come calling. At Tulsa University, Todd Graham, a former Texas high school coach himself, was able to lure Morris away from the Cavaliers to become the offensive coordinator and associate head coach. Once again, Morris found himself in an up-and-coming program with a dynamic quarterback who had recently transferred from the University of Texas. His name: G.J. Kinne from Gilmer High School. Morris and Kinne partnered beautifully, and Tulsa went on to win 10 games, including an upset of Notre Dame, and Kinne was named Conference USA's Offensive Player of the Year for 2010.

Meanwhile, Lake Travis didn't miss a beat. Morris's top assistant, Hank Carter, was promoted to head coach, and the Cavaliers again went on to capture the 4A State Championship in 2010 and 2011. This marked five state titles in a row, and it was now crystal clear that the Cavaliers had the best football program in Texas.

***

Pine Tree High School was one of three school districts located in Longview. Dating back to the 1980s, it had a reputation for being less imposing than Longview High but much more sophisticated than the smaller Spring Hill. It had also been known as the district where the "new money" lived. With highly educated, high-income parents, the district's students consistently scored higher in state athletic and academic contests than did their neighboring schools. Teams in volleyball, basketball, baseball, and golf regularly won district championships and made the playoffs. Graduates of those programs were making a name for themselves on college campuses and beyond—but football was lagging.

For one, more kids specialized at Pine Tree. Not as many played multiple sports so fewer athletes who were talented in other realms trickled into football. Several credible coaches tried to go in and change the culture; but for whatever reason, the word on Pine Tree was that it just wasn't a football school. Since 1980, the football program had made the playoffs only three times and had never won more than seven games in a season.

In the late 2000s, more wealthy housing developments started going up in Longview, this time in the Spring Hill area. Slowly, Pine Tree's school district population started to become more economically diverse like its larger counterpart, Longview High.

Newly affluent Spring Hill, on the other hand, with its influx of wealth, was experiencing new local leadership and increased specialization from its students. As with Pine Tree, the overall gain in athletics was a loss to the football program. The team went from making the playoffs seven out of eight years in the first part of the 2000s to not making the playoffs at all from 2008-2013.

Meanwhile, Pine Tree was in the process of reimagining itself. In 2011, the school hired new superintendent, T.J. Farlar, who ushered in a $29.9 million bond referendum that funded a new football stadium. In 2013, the stadium was officially complete. Now, it just needed to find the right coach, and it set its sights on Lake Travis, which had captured the state title five years in a row. Over the winter break of 2013, Lake Travis lost assistant coach, David Collins, to Pine Tree, which hired him to lead the program. With that hire, the possibility of greatness came into view, and the district went all in on trying to get football participation numbers up and investing in facilities, all the while raiding every high school program they could to assemble one of the best coaching staffs in East Texas.

Collins proved a big get. In the spring offseason of 2014, kids were immediately drawn to him because he'd coached Baker Mayfield and several other future college quarterbacks. His presence notched up the quality of talent eager to play in his style: an exciting, high-scoring offense.

"When I first got to Lake Travis, I was a pure 'Air Raid' guy," said Collins in an interview with *East Texas Sports Network (ETSN)*. "I had studied [Mike] Leach, and [Hal] Mumme. Then, when I got to Lake Travis, I was obviously influenced by Coach Morris, and [Gus] Malzahn. Since then, I've tried to marry both systems."

In his first game as a new head coach, Collins put up 37 points against former district rival Jacksonville High. Unfortunately, the Indians scored 62 in response. Collins was eager to show that he and his team were unphased. Plus, their next game was going to be against a smaller opponent. Pine Tree played 5A, and next week's opponent was class 4A's Gilmer Buckeyes.

"We're not rivals or anything," said Gilmer's Blake Lynch. "But because they're so close to us we definitely wanted to beat them. And because they were a bigger school, they looked down on us, so we wanted to let them know we can compete with anybody, 5A or 6A."

"Pine Tree was an up-and-coming program," recalled McLane Carter. "But we could've played 6A football that year. We weren't going to have any problem with them."

The confidence the Buckeye players had was evident from the first play of the game, when senior Kris Boyd took the opening kickoff 88 yards to the end zone effortlessly outrunning the Pine Tree defense. Boyd knew that the new Texas Tech head coach, Kliff Kingsbury, was in attendance to see the phenom in person, and he let him know that it was about to be a show.

"I remember watching Kris do that and being like, 'Holy Shit, he could play for Alabama right now,'" said Carter.

There was one hiccup on the end of the play though. Just as Boyd was about to make his last two strides to cross the goal line, he casually tossed the ball to the referee. But the referee avoided the toss and let it bounce around in the end zone. Boyd's Buckeye teammates noticed the avoidance and quickly realized that Boyd had not crossed the goal line when he let go of the ball. It was a fumble, and another Buckeye player jumped on it to get the touchdown.

Traylor was furious and quickly let his star player know that his lack of attention to detail almost cost them a touchdown.

The very next offensive series, after Gilmer forced a Pine Tree turnover, Boyd again bore the brunt of Coach Traylor's displeasure.

"My little brother had gotten tackled by like four dudes close to our sideline, and two of them did some extra stuff," said Boyd. "So, I'm on the sideline watching, and I run in and grab two of them and start throwing them down. Coach Traylor ran over and said he didn't care what they did, you don't act like that."

"He also basically told me, 'I don't care who's here to see you. Go sit down.'"

Boyd was benched for the rest of the first half. It was a clear message to the rest of the team.

"Mind you, Coach Kingsbury was there to see Kris," said Lynch. "I remember that just stuck out to me so much, because Coach Traylor didn't care about Texas Tech. This was *his* program and this was the way they were going to do things. You're a part of the team, you're not bigger than the team. Being new, I was like *wow*. This whole organization is really serious, and it's really a team."

Even with one of its star players on the bench, Gilmer continued its dominance, finding the end zone on its next five possessions after an opening drive field goal.

Lynch continued to show his versatility by catching a touchdown, throwing two more, and being a threat on the ground. Carter also maintained his poise and accuracy going 10-15 in the air for 168 yards and two touchdowns.

Most importantly, Boyd came back in the second half and added 56 yards receiving on offense and also lined up on defense to make sure that Pine Tree's coach knew that the Lake Travis passing attack wasn't going to work here. The Pirates managed just four yards through the air and completed only one pass the entire night. At the end of the game, the final score read Gilmer 68, Pine Tree 20.

"I didn't trip on any of that stuff," said Boyd. "Anything Coach Traylor does, it was always for the best. He was always hard on discipline."

Boyd's posture of humility and determination as a senior was a testament to his own ambition. He knew he was destined for bigger things, and he wanted to make his family proud. His attitude exemplified what Traylor wanted in his football program, excellence on the field and off.

Born in Henderson, Boyd was raised back and forth between South Dallas and East Texas in his early years and moved to Gilmer in the third grade. Soon after, at age 11, he lost his father and moved into the "300 apartments" with his grandma, uncle, and four siblings.

"It was a project apartment," said Boyd. "We lived right on Highway 300 across from the junior high. My grandma always kept us in the church house, which was huge. She saved me."

Another outlet for the young boy was football. Shortly after his father died, Boyd asked to sign up for Gilmer's youth football team. He was a natural and led his team to the league Super Bowl during his first year.

"I was on the front page of the newspaper. It kind of planted a seed that I knew I would do something better. I think others even knew I was headed for something great," said Boyd.

"His dad had passed, and his mom had some issues, so his grandmother basically raised him," said Coach Keith Tate. "He had his struggles with various things. But he always knew what he wanted to do. I never had any doubts about Kris Boyd."

The young prodigy continued to progress in junior high, dominating the area's competition at his grade level. As a high school freshman, he moved up to varsity, a massive jump, but Traylor knew he could more than handle it.

"Coach Traylor used to come and pick me up to take me to school every day my freshman year," said Boyd. "We'd joke around all of the time. I really felt like he treated me like his son. He was tough on me too, which I needed. Sometimes he'd say, 'Don't make me get on your ass' or 'You're better than that,'" said Boyd, laughing.

"He knew my dreams though, and we'd talk about them every morning. He wanted to see every one of his players accomplish their dreams, too. Before I got to the high school, I'd see Stump Godfrey and him talk and hug before games. I remember in warm-ups he'd always go by and hug his players. He did it to every person. I remember thinking, 'I can't wait until that's me.'"

Their early bond would prove to be crucial to Boyd's life when his grandmother died during his sophomore year.

"I remember we had a big game that week," said Boyd. "Coach Traylor told me I could miss the preparation stuff and go see my grandmother, and I'd still be fine to play. That was so important to me. I got to be with her at the end."

Sophomore year was also Boyd's coming out party for the college recruiting circuit. Gary Patterson's TCU Horned Frogs were the first to offer him that year. The next year, as a junior, he was on the radar of nearly every major college program.

"Junior year was big for me, but it was big for all of us. We thought we were going to win state that year. Then we lost to Argyle. I remember after we lost that one, I told myself I was going to do everything possible to make sure we reached our goal of a championship," said Boyd.

His coaches noticed a change in intensity after his junior year too.

"His senior year you could just tell that he was going to be a player," added assistant coach Kurt Traylor. "I mean he was a player, but he decided to be a player's player."

"Obviously the ability was there and always was," said coach Matt Turner. "He kind of took it to another level because he really started investing in teammates, not just himself. He grew as a man, and, as he grew, he helped the team grow."

His leadership was especially going to be needed when the Buckeyes headed to Tatum to play the Eagles, their toughest non-district opponent. It was time to be tested.

Now widely known for his confidence, Traylor had made quite the splash in 2001, his second year in command, when he predicted that the Buckeyes would not only make the playoffs, but they'd also win district for the first time in 10 years. Again, it went down to Gilmer versus Tatum.

Keeping it close through the first half, the Eagles once again looked like they were going to come away with the win when they scored a third quarter touchdown and safety and allowed Gilmer to only run four plays in the period.

But the Buckeyes rallied in the fourth behind quarterback Clint Quinn's third touchdown of the game. Now trailing 24-21, late in the fourth quarter, all Tatum had to do was take care of the ball and run out the clock.

"We called our last time out, and we told the guys when they come out all we got to do is hold him up, strip him, and then let's go," said Traylor. "And then we did it."

Sure enough, Tatum's Chris Shelton took the quarterback's handoff and was stopped and stripped by Gilmer defenders. Don Griffin picked up the fumble for the Buckeyes and returned it 62 yards for the go-ahead touchdown.

Gilmer claimed the victory and the district championship. At the time, it was also a culture win that demonstrated that Traylor's plan was working.

But would that success over Tatum continue? In 2004, the Eagles brought in Andy Evans to be its new head coach. Evans was a young, successful coach from the Southeast Texas region. Raised in Barbers Hill and Anahuac as the son of a coach, he got his first head job at East Chambers and invested nine years of his life turning the program into a consistent winner. When the Tatum job opened, it was just too good to turn down.

***

In the 1970s, Texas Utilities Company moved to Tatum to build Martin Creek Lake, an electrical power generating plant. In the process, it also strip-mined thousands of acres for lignite to fire its steam plant—and it was found in abundance. The local school district was the beneficiary, implementing massive school improvements in academics without raising taxes, to the delight of the community.

By the early 2000s, superintendent Dr. Dee Hart began reallocating a significant part of this funding to the athletic facilities. The field was upgraded to artificial turf coupled with a state-of-the-art press box featuring an elevator, which was the first of its kind in the region. Hart also built an indoor practice facility, which even most college programs didn't have at the time.

Tatum had always had talent. But for whatever reason, they were in a rut in the early 2000s, producing seasons with only seven or eight wins, total—a good number for some programs, but not for Tatum. Evans understood that, and he went to work when he took over as head football coach.

During his first four seasons as head coach, Tatum averaged just over 13 wins a year, won two state championships, and played for another one. It was one of the best runs in the state at the time.

The Eagles dipped a little bit in talent during the next few years, but they soon rose back to a level where they were in the conversation for the state championship. Anyone could tell that with one glance at the roster. It was filled with the names of families that had spawned generations of outstanding football talent, and the Eagles knew that with this team they could compete with anyone. The upcoming game against Gilmer was going to be a great test.

"Tatum-Gilmer has been a great rivalry for years, so I expect it to be a great ball game," said Traylor to *ETSN* the week before the match. "I imagine they're fast as always."

The contest was named Game of the Week by several area publications. Eagle Stadium was full of fans from both teams because the expectation was that the game was going to be a nail-biter.

Someone just forgot to tell Gilmer's Blake Lynch to be concerned.

"This was the game when we figured out who Blake Lynch was," said McLane Carter.

Having played the Eagles during his three previous years at Troup, the senior transfer entered the game with a little more focus than usual. This game was personal.

"They're the team I broke my arm against when I was at Troup," said Lynch. "They didn't like me. They also thought Gilmer recruited me, so they had a lot to say about me."

Lynch adopted the mantra that actions are louder than words; and on the first offensive play of the game for the Buckeyes, Carter threw a screen pass to Lynch, who then took it 50 yards for a touchdown. Lynch's teammates fed off his focus and were inspired by his mission to prove himself against his old nemesis.

By halftime, the score read Gilmer 27, Tatum 7. The momentum was fully on the visiting team's side. Evans, a seasoned coach who was a masterful motivator for his team, knew they weren't out of it yet. They just had to get back to their game plan.

On the opening drive to start the second half, the Eagles responded to their coach's game plan and marched 69 yards down the field, capped by a 22-yard pass from quarterback J.D. Traylor to Deyanta Roberson. The score now read 27-14. There was life on the Eagle sideline.

Gilmer then received the ball; and after approaching midfield, Tatum's Devon Boyd recovered a fumble from the Buckeyes and ran it all the way down deep into Gilmer territory. Three plays later, the Eagles scored again. The lead was now down to six points.

"I was like, oh crap, we actually have to play now," said Carter.

It was a strange feeling for the Buckeyes. They had won their first two games by a combined score of 123-36. There was tension in the air, but their senior transfer demonstrated his cool, confidence once again.

In the ensuing series, Lynch caught a pass from Carter for a 42-yard gain, and then followed that up a few plays later with a short-yard touchdown. Gilmer reclaimed its two-touchdown lead.

Tatum responded again, this time with a four-minute drive that finished with a one-yard touchdown rush by the quarterback. The lead was back to only a single touchdown. The Eagles just needed to capitalize on one turnover to make things really interesting.

They initially got their chance after recovering a fumble, but then Kris Boyd saved his team with an interception in the end zone. The ball positioning deep in Buckeye territory was problematic though. If another turnover were to happen, Tatum would be in scoring position.

Sure enough, on the very next play, Gilmer fumbled in its own end zone, and Tatum's Boyd recovered the ball for the game-tying touchdown.

The home crowd was electric. It was anyone's game.

Gilmer orchestrated a drive on its next possession, which lasted more than five minutes, and got all the way down to the Tatum 15; however, on fourth down, they elected to go for it rather than try for the field goal. McLane Carter, who had struggled the second half, threw an incomplete pass.

Tatum went to work gaining enough yardage to get them back to midfield. The Buckeye defense again came to the rescue, forcing a turnover on downs to get the ball back one last time with 2:12 left to play in the game.

Finally, this was all the Buckeyes needed. After advancing deep into Tatum territory, Gilmer's staff called a fake screen-and-go to Lynch. Carter delivered it perfectly for the game-winning touchdown with 26 seconds left.

"It was like a walk off," said Carter.

"They had been biting on the screens all night," said Lynch. "We decided to run a fake and I was wide open. My quarterback put it right on the money, and I just came down with the catch."

Lynch had put on a show. He'd scored five times that night, three times rushing the ball and two catching it. His teammates were in awe.

"We all saw it that night," said Carter. "We've got another guy who can take over a game by himself."

Yet, even with that victory, it was a night that exposed some weaknesses for the Buckeyes. Gilmer had fumbled the ball three times in the second half and blown a 20-point lead. Traylor knew they needed a game like this to see what they had in the tank. Tatum had pushed them to the limit.

"You've gotta give the kids credit," said Traylor. "They found a way to win. Whenever you play good people it's better for you, and we'll be better for this."

Blake Lynch (#9) catches a pass from McLane Carter to beat the Tatum Eagles 41-35. Lynch, who transferred to Gilmer before the season began, scored five touchdowns on the night. (Courtesy of Ruel Felipe)

Scott Surratt, long-time head coach of the Carthage Bulldogs, is known as one of the best coaches in the history of Texas High School Football. He and Jeff Traylor built two of the best programs in the state, and a great friendship grew as a result of their mutual respect for one another. (*News-Journal*/Michael Cavazos)

"It's not our fault if another team can't stop us."
--Blake Lynch

Chapter 10: Who's the BEAST?

After advancing to 3-0 in 2014, the Buckeyes focused their attention on one of the area's most historic programs, the Daingerfield Tigers. The previous season the Tigers had slipped in the quarterfinals to New Boston, but they were still only two years removed from being in the 2A Division I State Championship game.

Daingerfield had talent stretching back to the 1960s, when Bill Lane was leading the program, but it took two decades for the program to win state championships in 1983 and 1985, the era of Coach Dennis Alexander. They were *the* team in East Texas during this time, and Jeff Traylor knew them all too well.

"Growing up in Gilmer, it was always them and Gladewater," said Traylor. "Both of them always had our number, and we viewed them equally, but Daingerfield always had the edge and the championships to show it."

Even though he grew up on the losing end of most of these battles, Traylor never viewed either program as out of reach.

"There really wasn't that much of a talent disparity between Daingerfield, Gilmer, and Gladewater," he said.

"During my senior year as a Gilmer student, we actually beat Gladewater, but Daingerfield always owned us. That was the hardest thing when I went to coach at Gilmer for us to get over. Our entire community needed to get over that mental hurdle."

In 2001, Traylor's second year at the helm, Gilmer finally beat Daingerfield. But in 2002, they ended their season losing a heartbreaker to them in the playoffs.

"We outplayed them, too," said Traylor. "We ran a Quarterback Power on the one-yard line. They knocked it out of our hands, and then they took it ninety-nine yards for a touchdown. We still just weren't mentally ready to beat Daingerfield in such a high-stakes game."

Then in 2003, Gilmer again faced Daingerfield in the first round of the playoffs.

"They were number one in the state, and we played our best game of the year. Beat them 43-0," said Traylor. "That was the game when we became for real. That's when everybody in East Texas agreed that our program was legit. It was over for Daingerfield from then on."

Randy McFarlin was Daingerfield's head coach during Traylor's initial years at Gilmer. Highly respected, McFarlin had raised the Tigers to a level that they hadn't seen since the Dennis Alexander days, averaging nine wins a year over a six-year period, and they had even qualified for the 1998 3A state championship game.

But in 2004, a growing 4A school district in the Tyler area, Whitehouse, plucked McFarlin to guide its football program. Whitehouse didn't have nearly the tradition and history of Daingerfield, and it stood in the shadow of neighboring powers, John Tyler and Tyler Lee. But McFarlin relished the challenge and saw the school's potential. After nine successful years at the helm, McFarlin grew Whitehouse into one of the most respected programs in the area before leaving in 2012. McFarlin earned additional acclaim, too, for mentoring

Whitehouse quarterback Patrick Mahomes, perhaps the best quarterback to ever come out of East Texas.

McFarlin was the last Tigers coach to beat the Buckeyes during Traylor's tenure at Gilmer. Even when the Tigers won three straight state championships in class 2A from 2008 to 2010 under Barry Bowman, they always had one blemish on their regular season record. The Buckeyes beat them every time.

As the 2014 season started, Traylor looked forward to keeping his winning streak against Dangerfield during a season rematch that fall.

The Dangerfield game only bolstered Traylor's confidence. By halftime the score was Gilmer 47, Daingerfield 2. It was the script the Buckeyes had wholeheartedly expected to write. Kris Boyd scored three times in the first half on three different running plays, Blake Lynch scored on a 61-yard run and later tossed another touchdown to Quinn Fluellen, and McLane Carter simply enjoyed managing the game with all the talent in the world in his backfield.

"We were on cruise control," said Carter. "Just total domination."

The contest was such a washout that the Daingerfield announcer made a plea for mercy, unaware that he was on a hot mic.

"I remember him saying, 'We need to get this game over. It's getting out of hand,'" said Blake Lynch with a laugh. "Daingerfield had always had some serious athletes. And when we beat a program like theirs by 50-60, we knew we had something special."

The final score: Gilmer 61, Daingerfield 9. The Buckeyes were now 4-0 and ready to take on their last non-district opponent, the defending 4A state champion Carthage Bulldogs.

In fall 2014, Carthage and Gilmer were two of the best, if not *the* best, programs in all East Texas. During the prior decade, each had played in four state championship games, with Gilmer winning two of them and Carthage winning all four. The communities were proud, the players were talented, and there was an immense amount of respect between the two staffs. But there was also a rivalry that had ascended all the way up to the top of each program, and East Texans loved to debate the question, "Who's better, Gilmer's Jeff Traylor or Carthage's Scott Surratt?"

Scott Surratt hailed from Linden and had played quarterback and running back for the Linden-Kildare Tigers, but his best sport was baseball. His father, Ray, had coached hundreds of young kids in Linden's youth baseball league and passed along this love of the game to his three sons, but Scott advanced the farthest. After graduating from high school, he played baseball at East Texas Baptist University with the hope of getting into coaching after he graduated.

"I knew if I wasn't going to be a major league player, then coaching was what I wanted to do," said Surratt.

He realized his ambition when he began his career at Redwater as head baseball coach, and he also coached football there. After a year, he was hired by Little Cypress-Mauriceville (LCM), located in Orange, to be its head baseball coach where he grew close to another staff assistant, Barry Norton.

"Scott and I lived together, we coached together, then we both left after he'd been there for two years," said Norton in an interview with *The Texarkana Gazette*. "It was one of those deals where we talked every weekend about strategy and tactics, how you do this and how you do that. And we always knew if I ever got a head coaching job, Scott was going to come and be my offensive coordinator."

After leaving LCM, Norton went to Port Arthur Jefferson, and then he was hired at West Orange-Stark High School, working under the formidable head coach, Dan Ray Hooks, before landing his first head job at Texas High in Texarkana several years later.

Surratt then came back home to Linden and took over the head baseball job at Linden-Kildare High School (L-K) while also serving as offensive coordinator for the football team. But the football bug had finally bitten Surratt. He wanted to be a head football coach, and that meant gaining experience.

"When Scott got to L-K, you saw him start to grow as a football coach, especially after he became responsible for the offense," Norton said.

After five years serving his hometown, Surratt took the passing coordinator position for one year at a larger high school, Waxahachie, before Barry Norton tapped him to be the offensive coordinator for the Texas High Tigers.

In the friends' first year teaming there, the Tigers captured their first district title in 15 years. The duo never looked back. During the eight seasons when Surratt served as Norton's offensive coordinator, they won seven district championships, had three undefeated regular seasons, and triumphed at the 2002 4A state championship. Surratt had proven he was one of the elite offensive minds in the state, and this was no more evident than in his final year with the Tigers, when he coached senior quarterback Ryan Mallett.

Mallett had always been Surratt's guy. When his star pupil was only an eighth grader, Surratt invited him to informal workouts for Tiger quarterbacks—but Surratt didn't let on that Mallett wasn't even in high school yet.

"I introduced him as a junior," said Surratt. "Sure enough, he starts throwing and the rest of them were like, 'uh oh, we got some competition.' This was an eighth grader. Man, he could always spin it."

Leading the Tigers to an undefeated regular season in his senior year, Mallett delivered one of the single greatest individual seasons in the school's history. He threw for over 3,000 yards, had 33 touchdowns, and only three interceptions. Although the Tigers didn't make it to the state title that year, Mallett delivered one of the most memorable games in Texas High's history, in a matchup with Highland Park.

After the previous year's disappointing 38-31 playoff loss to eventual state champion Highland Park, led by All-American senior quarterback Matthew Stafford, Mallett knew they might get a shot at revenge the following year against the state of Texas's most famous high school program. In Shreveport's Independence Stadium, with a chance to go to the regional finals, Surratt devised a game plan that allowed Mallett to put up 42 points on the Highland Park defense. The point total was more than enough to get the win, and the performance solidified Mallett's spot as the best quarterback in the state.

Already committed to play for Lloyd Carr at the University of Michigan, Mallett was named Gatorade Player of the Year in the State of Texas and rated the number four overall player in the nation by *Rivals.com*. His long-time mentor beamed with pride.

"He's like a son to me," said Surratt.

In addition to the sports reporters, there was another person in the crowd that day who left Independence Stadium extremely impressed. Carthage High alumnus George Allison had been at the game. The son of Carthage school district's superintendent, Reba Allison, he convinced her to hire Surratt—one of the most important decisions of her tenure.

"He'd followed me since I was Ryan Mallet's coordinator, and he had done his research on me and even came to see us play Highland Park in Shreveport," Surratt said. "Luckily, we played well when he came."

***

Carthage was a blue-collar, oil field community that had fallen on hard times. The school had been identified as low-performing academically by the state; most of the school's sports, especially football, were also unimpressive. Compounding the town's woes, in December 2006, a natural gas leak had erupted on the outskirts of Carthage, forcing over a hundred residents from their homes.

"There were so many negative things going on when we came," said Surratt. "We literally had to go in and change the culture."

Surratt started this monumental job the day after spring break and quickly sought ways to build trust in a program that was on its fourth head football coach in seven years.

First, he met with the entire team to introduce himself.

"I know most of you guys have already had three head coaches already. Seniors, I'm the third head coach of your high school career. I know it's going to be hard to get your trust, but I'm going to be here every day trying to earn it."

Surratt's next task was getting the holdovers from the previous staff to buy in.

"I remember talking to one of the junior high coaches when I got here, and I asked him about the eighth-grade class. He said, 'We've got one player, and then the rest of them aren't any good. This is the worst group we've ever had,' and I looked at him straight in the eye and said, 'The next time I ask you about these kids, you better have something positive to say, or we're going to find somebody else who can.'"

"He then privately asked my defensive coordinator who I had brought with me, 'Is he serious?' And Garrett (Morgan) told him, 'Dang right, he's serious.'"

The next step was getting the entire town on board, and, by chance, Surratt was afforded just the right venue to make his sales pitch to the Carthage faithful.

"When I got here in the spring, a bond was being voted on, and everybody said it was fifty-fifty whether it's going to pass or not. The stadium they had was awful, and they badly needed something new. So, I hear that there's only a fifty-fifty chance, and I'm saying to myself, 'You've got to be kidding me.'"

Surratt swung into action.

"So, we go around the community talking to folks, and then we got some help from this guy who owned his own construction company. We rented out the Texas Country Music Hall of

Fame, which is here in Carthage, for about a hundred dollars an hour, and we invited the whole community in. And this old boy with the construction company said, 'If you get them here, I will feed them barbeque all day for free.'"

"We advertised a free barbeque on the radio and in the paper, and it looked like the entire community had come. All I did was reassure them that the bond was not going to raise their taxes. I had a big PowerPoint that just said, 'It's a win, win, win.' I let them know that we were going to hold the players accountable for their grades and we'd help the overall school. We won their trust."

"Sure enough, the bond passed by like seventy-five percent. I was nervous as a cat," said Surratt. "We've had six more bonds since I've been here, and the least number we've had on any of them is eighty-one percent. Heck, we got ninety percent on the full-size indoor practice field. We now have the biggest scoreboard screen in the state of Texas, and it passed at eighty-one percent. But it all started that day at the Texas Country Music Hall of Fame, and we backed up that we could win, too."

In Surratt's debut season, Carthage went undefeated in district play and captured the school's first district title in 13 years.

"We ended up losing in the playoffs to Liberty Hill that year, and they were the eventual state champions. We played them better than anyone else had, and we actually had a great shot at winning. After that, we really got the town behind us—when we went on to win three in a row."

From 2008 to 2010, Surratt and the Carthage Bulldogs won three state championships in a row just as the Daingerfield Tigers had, but Carthage won in the highly competitive class 3A. In East Texas's Class 3A, there was a period of success and competition that was unprecedented in the region. Carthage won from 2008-2010, Gilmer won in 2009, Henderson won in 2010, and Chapel Hill won in 2011. All these schools were located so close to each other that sometimes they were even in the same district. The local online message boards were lit up with debates among fans arguing about who had the best coach. Most of the time though, it was a two-horse race. You were either a Traylor guy or a Surratt guy, but, for two nemeses, the two coaches had uncannily similar backgrounds.

Surratt grew up in a small East Texas town (Linden); Traylor grew up in a small East Texas town (Gilmer). Surratt had two brothers; Traylor had two brothers. Surratt played college ball at an East Texas University (ETBU); Traylor played ball at an East Texas University (SFA). Surratt had been a head baseball coach; Traylor had been a head basketball coach. Surratt had been mentored by Barry Norton at Texas High; Traylor had been mentored by Danny Long at Jacksonville. Surratt had mentored Ryan Mallett; Traylor had mentored Josh McCown. Surratt had led Carthage to its first state title; Traylor had led Gilmer to its first state title.

And each matchup of their programs was a head-to-head battle. But with that fierce competition came incredible opportunities for the players' growth.

In 2008, the first time Surratt coached against Traylor, Carthage escaped with a 31-28 win over Gilmer in the fourth round of the playoffs on its journey to win state. Round two happened two years later, when both teams were playing in the same district and Carthage simply had too much talent. The Bulldogs overmatched the Buckeyes 38-21 to claim the district title. The following year, in the 2011 season, Gilmer returned the favor and won round three by a score of 39-36 over the Bulldogs to retake the district crown. The game still ranks as one of Traylor's proudest moments as a coach and a parent as his son, Jordan, had to engineer a late-game victory.

Matt Turner's son, Luke, and Traylor's son, Jordan, were best friends and both seniors on the Buckeye football team that had triumphed over the Bulldogs that season. To say that their families were poised for a special year would be a huge understatement.

Gilmer had begun the year 6-0, when Luke was the starting quarterback and featured player on the team. Jordan was Luke's backup at quarterback, but he also served as the starting tight end. The offense was averaging 42 points a game leading up to the Carthage matchup, and the Buckeyes were dead set on putting an end to the Bulldogs reign over the region.

After completing a two-point conversion to put Gilmer up 36-29 with 5:36 left in the game, Turner came up limping. It turned out that after landing wrong on a bootleg pass, he'd broken one of the bones in his foot and was sidelined. Luke had started 49 consecutive games prior to the Carthage game.

"He got hurt on a freak play," said Traylor. "As many times as we ran him, he got hurt on a bootleg pass, so it's kind of ironic."

Carthage quickly tied the contest in a little over a minute, and Jordan Traylor was thrust into the role of quarterback with 4:30 remaining on the clock and a tie game.

"Whenever you lose anybody, everybody's gotta step up. That's in any walk of life—work, coaching ball, school—when you lose somebody, everybody's gotta do a little more."

Jordan did exactly that, leading his team on a 12-play, 60-yard drive all the way down to the Carthage 14-yard line with seconds remaining. The Buckeyes' Pablin Olivares then stepped in and booted a 31-yard field goal to win the game 39-36.

"We've coached a lot of great high school games, but it's probably the best one we've had in Gilmer. That was a dandy," Traylor said.

The same Gilmer team performed perfectly to end the 2011 regular season and went on to advance all the way to the quarterfinals before losing to Argyle. Jordan and Luke were rewarded for their play by winning co-MVPs of the district. The other senior to take home a superlative was Darrion Pollard, who was named Offensive MVP. He was Desmond's older brother.

"I remember some people making comments about whether Jordan was the right person for the position," said his mother, Cari Traylor. "And I sometimes wondered if he was the right player, but I knew that Jeff wouldn't put him in if he couldn't go. The games were really exciting, but there was a lot of pressure on the players, and Jordan stepped up and proved himself."

Surratt held a 2-1 series advantage over Traylor leading up to their next game, and he was coming off Carthage's fourth state championship run in 2013, but he wasn't cocky.

"We believe complacency kills," says Surratt. "We have a response when people ask, 'What's your favorite ring?' We say, 'It's the next one.' We're very proud of what we've done, but we don't dwell on it."

***

The local country radio station *did* dwell on it. KYKX was sponsoring a Saturday night Game of the Week series hosted at Longview's Lobo Stadium throughout the regular season. It was the brainchild of Harlen the Sports Guy and Pigskin Bob, the popular co-hosts of the region's Friday Night Scoreboard Show.

"Several years ago, there was a game I really wanted to see," said Harlen. "But since we go on the air at eight-thirty p.m. on Fridays, we don't get to see very many games. And I thought: man, wouldn't it be great if every week there was one great game played on Saturday so everyone who wanted to see it could go. About an hour later, the light bulb went off: *Harlen, you can do this*!! It took several years of planning and scheduling to make it work, but we did it."

"I thought Harlen was crazy at first," said Bob. "But then I realized that these Saturday games could turn out to be the Monday Night Football of East Texas high school football!"

The Game of the Week series began in 2012 and featured high-profile regional matchups called by the two KYKX broadcasters, with live radio sponsorships from the likes of local country singer, Neal McCoy.

***

A top broadcast of the 2014 season was Gilmer versus Carthage—and it was a revealing one.

While the contest *seemed* like it could potentially be another instant classic, the fact of the matter was that Carthage wasn't nearly as talented that year as Gilmer. The entire fan base would soon see and hear that clearly for themselves.

After winning the opening coin toss, the Buckeyes elected to receive. On the first play from scrimmage, McLane Carter threw a simple dump pass to Kris Boyd in the flat. As was the case in previous games, Boyd turned ordinary into extraordinary. He made the first group of tacklers miss near the sideline and then turned it back towards the middle of the field with blockers leading the way for a 48-yard touchdown.

"Going into that week, Coach Traylor was coaching us super hard," said Lynch. "'This is Carthage! We go back and forth every single year. This is our year!' He just went on that we're not losing to them. I remember going into the game—it was super serious."

The attitude of their leader was reflected in the ensuing plays by defensive coordinator Todd Barr's Black Flag defense.

After coming back with a strong Carthage offensive drive that led the Bulldogs all the way down to the Gilmer 20-yard line, quarterback Jarod Blissett ran a sneak to the Gilmer five, before being stripped and recovered by Nick Smith. Smith then took it 95 yards for the Buckeye touchdown. The score was now 14-0.

On the ensuing possession for Carthage, Blissett again turned the ball over, this time through the air, when defensive back Devin Smith intercepted the pass and took it 25 yards for another Gilmer touchdown.

Amazingly, the Black Flag defense still wasn't finished. After catching a nine-yard reception, receiver Justin Clough fumbled the ball, and this time Blake Lynch snatched it up and took it 75 yards for another Buckeye touchdown.

With 3:55 left to play in the first quarter, the score read Gilmer 27, Carthage 0.

"I've coached for twenty-five years and never seen that and doubt I'll see it again the rest of my life," said Traylor to *ETSN* after the game. "I've got to give credit to our kids for the strips, scoops and scores. So far, it's just been one of those years for Scott Surratt, where he's just snake bitten like that. It happens sometimes in this business."

Meanwhile, the Gilmer offense stayed off the field until the 10:11 mark in the second quarter.

"I was trying to find a way not to get cold," said McLane Carter. "It was like eighty-five degrees in October, and I'm getting cold. I barely played."

Carter eventually did get in on the action before the half came to a close when he connected with Chase Tate on a 63-yard touchdown strike. Lynch delivered the next touchdown pass on the Buckeyes ensuing drive when he tossed Quinn Fluellen a four-yard touchdown pass to make the score 41-11 at the half.

"We were the best programs in the area, and we spanked them," said Carter. "We all remembered the lesson we learned in the Tatum game, when they were able to come back and almost win. We sure weren't going to let that happen in *this* game."

And the Buckeyes were true to their word.

The final score read Gilmer 58, Carthage 14. It was a dominant performance by Gilmer on East Texas's version of Monday Night Football. Traylor had also evened up his series with Surratt at two wins apiece.

"When you play a team as good as Carthage and a coach as good as Coach Surratt, you're just glad to be ahead," Traylor said.

They were more than glad, though. They were getting better, and the players could feel it.

"We were growing," said Carter. "We were growing mentally. We were making big stops. Our offense was playing better. We were communicating better with each other. We were playing harder."

"The camaraderie between everybody was fantastic too," said Lynch. "Like, we were cool on the field, but we were becoming even closer off it. McLane lived like 200 yards from the fieldhouse, so there would be 10-20 guys over at his house after practice and after Friday night games. It was cool."

The first part of Gilmer's schedule was officially over. The Buckeyes had just beaten three of the region and state's winningest programs from the last 15 years, and they had made it look easy. Their first five opponents in their district lacked their talent, so they would have to challenge themselves internally for the remainder of the regular season.

Gilmer's veteran staff knew the cardinal rule of handling success—don't get distracted. Coaches like Metzel, Turner, Barr, Tate, Coleman, and the Traylor brothers kept the team grounded. And that was reinforced by the player leadership: Boyd, Carter, and Lynch.

"It was crazy, we were beating teams by forty to fifty points, and then we'd show up to practice like nothing happened," said Lynch. "It was like we just expected it to happen. I don't know how to explain it. We'd beat them, and then we'd go back to practice and grind hard and have fun."

The margin of victory was allowing other players to get time on the field, and the expectation was that they were to repeat the success of the starters.

"I've heard Coach Traylor say that some coaches get mad at him for running up the score, and he told one of them that his twos and threes practice just as hard as the ones. So, when they got in there, he was going to give them the opportunity no matter what."

"I always respected that. I mean, I understand both sides," said Lynch. "But if you grind just like everybody else, you should get the opportunity to make plays. It's not our fault that another team can't stop us."

The Boyd brothers, Demarco (#5) and Kris (#21), carry Gilmer's infamous Black Flag with them as they run onto the field. The idea for the flag came from long-time defensive coordinator Todd Barr. (Courtesy of Ruel Felipe)

"I still remember when Coach Traylor came up to me when I was a kid. He said I was going to do something that my brother never did. I asked what that was, and he told me, 'You're going to win a state championship.'"
--McLane Carter

Chapter 11: Hot Streak

In February 2014, the Buckeyes caught a major break.

The UIL once again realigned the districts, placing Gilmer in 4A's Division II, which also included Melissa, Canton, Bullard, Emory Rains, and Nevada Community, not exactly household names in the Texas high school football world. Gilmer was the largest school in this classification, just squeaking through with 685 students. The cut-off was 686.

Finally, the Buckeyes were sprung from the District of Doom and four years in the buzzsaw, playing against formidable schools like Carthage, Henderson, Gladewater, Chapel Hill, and Kilgore. When he heard the news, Coach Jeff Traylor was relieved and responded with his typical humor.

"On one hand, I hate it because those are some great rivalries and great games," he said to *The Longview News-Journal*. "On the other side of it, if you want to keep your job it's probably a good idea you don't play those guys."

They left the brutal district with their heads held high. They had prevailed winning two district championships and coming in second in the other two years. But the dip in competition would be the ultimate test of how mature and focused the Buckeyes' upperclassmen really were. After going a perfect 5-0 for the non-district portion of their schedule, then came the district matchups—a far cry from archrivals like Gladewater, Carthage, and Henderson.

The Buckeyes opened district play on the road at Melissa, and running back Kris Boyd immediately let his coaches know that the team was more than fine. Rushing for 168 yards and four touchdowns on just nine carries, Boyd led Gilmer to a 63-0 district-opening win. The trouncing almost wasn't fair. The score was 49-0 at halftime.

***

Gilmer followed that performance by beating Canton in its home opener 70-0. The score was 21-0 in the first 90 seconds.

It was also homecoming and Yamboree weekend in Gilmer, and the program was honoring the 2004 state championship team. It could not have gone any better.

"That home side was packed, people everywhere, it was awesome," said Traylor. "Fans have always been great to us, a great community that loves football. They're always supportive."

McLane Carter completed 11 of 15 passes for 237 yards and five touchdowns, all in the first half, with Boyd and Lynch each receiving two apiece. The senior quarterback was in complete control, and he was gaining confidence each week.

Still, Traylor was nervous about this much of a drop-off in competition.

"We've had some great good-on-good sessions, seven-on-seven, but we knew we'd need to be tested soon to see how we measured up against playoff-level teams," he said to *ETSN*.

But that test wasn't coming anytime soon. While Bullard was able to make the claim that they were the first district opponent to score on the Buckeyes, the Panthers only did it once and were then pummeled by a score of 49-7. This time Gilmer dominated with its ground game.

Kris Boyd and Blake Lynch accounted for four rushing touchdowns on the night, and Boyd's younger brother, Demarco, added two.

"I've talked about this with several other friends who have lived in this area their entire lives," said Gilmer High School principal Brian Bowman. "It's certainly the most talented team I've ever seen."

Gilmer had now outscored its first three district opponents 182-7. The numbers were outrageous enough to warrant discussions from locals across East Texas about how this team ranked against other historically great teams from the region.

***

But Gilmer couldn't just rest on the laurels of its current performance. It would have to earn its place in history. The "greatest season ever" conversations in East Texas always seemed to focus on three particular teams in their glory years: the Big Sandy Wildcats in 1975, the Pittsburg Pirates in 1980, and the Daingerfield Tigers in 1983. And those whose historical memory spans more than 50 years, also point out programs like the Prairie View Interscholastic League's (PVIL) Lufkin Dunbar teams of the 1960's in addition to the modern-day Tatum, Daingerfield, and Carthage rosters that could all boast of an age of when they won multiple championships and cemented dynasties.

East Texas's winningest programs from the mid-1970s to the early 1980s all shared a similar strategy. They lived and breathed a rough and gritty defense born of the blue-collar ethos in the Lone Star Steel region, a style of play that epitomized the toughness of the company's roughly 3,000 workers. The early 1980s added a new swagger to that grittiness. The company was booming after developing a new kind of casing for steel, oil, and gas wells, which resisted hydrogen sulfide corrosion, bringing in an annual revenue in excess of $70 million, more money than the community had ever seen.

The two teams that most embodied the region's newfound confidence were Pittsburg and Daingerfield.

Pittsburg set the standard first when its 1980 squad, led by head coach James Rust, posted a 15-0 state championship season in class 3A, showcasing a defense that allowed only 23 points the entire season. Even more impressive was that 14 of those points came against Mount Pleasant during week one, and the other seven came against Jacksonville in week four. That meant the defense did not allow another point during the other 13 games. The two points to make 23 total points came in the state championship game versus Van Vleck when the offense took a safety.

During this era, no one in East Texas, and potentially the entire state, had ever seen a defense like Pittsburg's. Their 12 shutouts were a record, and one that it seemed might hold up for the rest of time.

Unfortunately, the record held for only three years before it was broken by its rival, Daingerfield. Under its young, dynamic coach, Dennis Alexander, known as "D.A." to his familiars, the Tigers also played with a brand of toughness and excellence that matched the ethos of the land.

"We were coached so well," said Dangerfield cornerback Johnnie Hurndon in an interview with *Lone Star Preps*. "Coach Alexander had us prepared. He was such a special coach and motivator."

Alexander was a Kilgore native who left the Piney Woods for Rice University, a pick made in part for the school's excellent academics. With a brilliant mind and a passion for coaching football, Alexander eventually made it back to East Texas, where he took his first head coaching position at Hughes Springs. After four years, he transitioned over to Daingerfield and found success almost immediately.

D.A. produced a winner in five of his first six seasons; but it wasn't until 1982 that he got his first shot at the playoffs. The UIL only granted district champions a ticket to make the playoffs back then, and in 1982 he finally got his first gold ball. Daingerfield then took it to another level. During the next three years, the Tigers captured two state championships and had an overall record of 46-1-1. But even with that great three-year run, the 1983 team was held up as Alexander's masterpiece.

***

On a cold December day at Baylor's Floyd Casey Stadium in 1983, Daingerfield defeated Sweeney 42-0 in the 3A state championship game to cap off what was arguably the most dominant season ever recorded in Texas high school football history. The Tigers became the first Texas team to go 16-0 and set a national record for shutouts in a season at 14. Overall, they outscored their opponents 631-8, and the defense allowed only six of those points in a regular season game against Carthage.

"I think somebody fell down in the secondary, and they [Carthage] burned us for a 76-yard touchdown," said senior quarterback Doug Pittman to *The Fort Worth Star-Telegram*. "That pissed the defense off, and they blocked the extra point."

The defense, led by future NFL standout Eric Everett, was famous. They were the second Texas high school program in history that refused to yield even a single point in the playoffs. (Abilene was the first, in 1923.)

The Tigers won because they went full speed every day, unlike other teams that saved their juice for the games.

"Our practices were just as intense as the games," Everett said in the *Waco Tribune-Herald*. "It just sort of became second nature, and our players were at the top of the division, so we were practicing with the best, and the games became pretty easy. We never looked at it as a job; it was just fun."

They had fun all right. But they were also mean. Other teams genuinely feared playing them.

"Coach [Stan] Williams, my line coach, told me before every game to go out there and knock the snot out of them on the first play of the game and to let them know I'd be relentless," said Everett. "We just loved to play football. We'd go out and win, then get up the next day, go fishing, do our chores and then go out and win again."

***

Daingerfield and Pittsburg's successes were the byproduct of the overall success of the region; in contrast, Big Sandy's program didn't emanate from a town's success—it drove it. Before Jim Norman took over as the Wildcats' head football coach, mentoring such standouts as Lovie Smith and David Overstreet, the community was generally described as a "shriveled-up stop racked by hatred for race and religion. The school's facilities were abysmal; morale was even worse."

Big Sandy, Jeff Traylor's first coaching job, was where he learned about the spillover power of pride from a team into a community.

"We heard about Lovie Smith and Jim Norman and David Overstreet all the time when I was there," said Traylor. "They honored those guys. I emulated them my entire career."

***

Born in Tunica, Mississippi, in 1935, Big Sandy coach Jim Norman attended Hernando High School before earning his undergraduate degree from Delta State University. He went on to serve in the U.S. Army before embarking on his coaching career and took his first head coaching job at Big Sandy in 1970.

At the time, all Big Sandy had going for it was being known as the needlework capital of the South due to its two large suppliers of crochet kits and sewing patterns. The school had a low academic rating, and the local football team hadn't been to the playoffs since 1937. Not exactly a prime target for an up-and-coming coach.

In Norman's first year in charge, the Wildcats won only four games, but he achieved nearly the impossible when he brought equity and harmony to a team toxified by racial hatred. He began his tenure proclaiming that color would not matter. He then backed it up with who he played.

One story that gets retold often in Big Sandy circles recounts a moment early in Norman's career when he broke up a fight between a Black player and a White player. Legend has it that he took the two boys into his office, took out his pocketknife, and then made a small cut in each player's arm. As they both stood in silence and watched identical flows of red blood from their arms, Norman got his point across.

"The harmony on the football field is one big factor in the harmony in this whole town," superintendent Charles Penney told *Texas Monthly*.

Norman also got his program's numbers up by implementing a rule not to cut anyone who wanted to play. He knew kids and believed in his ability to motivate them, and he quickly developed a reputation for finding ways to give kids value.

"I remember a skinny old kid who kind of looked like an end but had two left feet," said Penney. "He had been cut the year before, but Coach somehow had him catching passes in no time."

Norman had shown his commitment to his new community, and now it was the town's turn to demonstrate its commitment to him. The next year, the town approved a 60 percent tax increase in order to finance school and football improvements, and Norman rewarded their trust by winning district the next two seasons and advancing to the playoffs.

Life in Big Sandy was improving, and it was about to get even better when two of the most gifted players to ever come through the East Texas region joined the varsity team. Their names: David Overstreet and Lovie Smith.

They were the perfect combination of talent. Overstreet, a once-in-a-generation running back who eventually went on to star at the University of Oklahoma and the NFL's Miami Dolphins; and Lovie Smith, a talented linebacker whose intellect for the game would set him apart later in his career as an NFL head coach. With those two now on varsity, Big Sandy didn't lose a game during the 1973-75 seasons and went on to capture three straight Class B state championships.

The capstone year for their dynasty was 1975, when they set the national scoring record. In 14 games, the Wildcats scored 824 points, while their opponents were held to a measly 15. Star running back David Overstreet scored 56 touchdowns and rushed for more than 3,000 yards.

"Every time he touched the ball, the odds were that he was going to score," said teammate Love Smith to *ETSN*. "Not that he might score. You were surprised when he didn't."

The team became iconic in small-town East Texas. In fact, they became so big that Coach Norman was elected Big Sandy's mayor, and he wasn't even on the ballot.

Never one to shy away from responsibility, Norman took on the role and even made his first order of business getting his own house off a septic tank and onto the city's sewer line.

"Dad actually took it very seriously," said David Norman, Jim's son.

He also had a sense of humor. After Big Sandy captured its third title in '75, the team was met by firetrucks and police cars flashing lights and starting the town's celebration.

Norman quipped, "I'd like to know where you got the budget to put on that kind of show."

Big Sandy's coach had a remarkable impact on a community as a whole and on Lovie Smith in particular.

"Every part of my career was affected by him in some form or fashion," said Lovie Smith. "Guys like him leave an impression, and he had the life I wanted."

After the '75 season, Smith accepted a scholarship to play football for the University of Tulsa, where he became a two-time All-American at linebacker. After failing to make an NFL roster, Smith was determined to become a coach like Norman. He started by working 10 assistant coaching jobs in high school, college, and the pros eventually becoming head coach of the NFL's Chicago Bears in 2004. Two years later, he became the first African American head coach to lead his team to a Super Bowl.

His old high school beamed with pride back in Texas.

"You want to know why the Bears are winning?" said Norman. "I guarantee you that it's because the first thing Lovie did was turn those players into a *team*."

***

Traylor shaped himself in the mold of Norman, revitalizing not only the Buckeyes but also Gilmer during his 15-year tenure there.

"You win and now every boy in the school wants to be a part of this," said Kerry Lane who grew up in Upshur County. "You can't convince me that the staff didn't completely change the school and town."

"If you looked at Gilmer back in 1999 and what it is today, it couldn't be more different. Gilmer now has nice homes, land for sale that costs money, and businesses that are going up."

With a more attractive town, the school became a magnet for students throughout the state.

"I've often been approached by families, from like the Dallas area who are relocating, and they'll tell me how they've heard about Gilmer's academic and football excellence," said principal Brian Bowman.

There was also another eerily similar comparison to Big Sandy. The 2014 Buckeyes could score like the 1975 Wildcats. For example, over a 14-game schedule, Big Sandy had averaged a little over 58 points a game, and through its first eight games Gilmer was averaging just a little over 58 points a game.

And while there was some concern among Traylor and his staff about maintaining focus during these lopsided contests, they knew that the team had a unified purpose of honoring the memory of Desmond Pollard, a beloved player who had passed away the previous spring.

This was especially crucial for the tail end of the season. The Buckeyes were heavily favored over its final two district opponents—and mental lapses could upend their goals.

"It kind of re-focused everyone. We were able to kick it into another level of execution after that," said Matt Turner.

"Kick it into another level of execution" was an understatement. In front of its home crowd, against a much less talented Nevada Community program, Gilmer scored eight touchdowns in 16 plays and 43 points in the first quarter. The final score read Gilmer 85, Nevada Community 15.

"They actually took one touchdown away that game," said Blake Lynch. "It would've been 92."

Gilmer's Big Three stayed right on script for its offensive production. Kris Boyd had three touchdowns, two on the ground and one on special teams; Blake Lynch caught two touchdowns and also had a fumble recovery and an interception; and McLane Carter threw for 255 yards on 7-8 passing with three touchdown passes.

"That class was loaded," said Keith Tate, "and they loved to play the game."

The staff was especially proud of the generosity of the star players when they went out of the game.

"I remember we would get all of the dudes' touchdowns, and then we would put in the backups, and our dudes are cheering them on," said Kerry Lane. "If you're not a part of it, you think they're trying to run up the score. But we were really just so excited that our backups were having some success."

For its final district game, Gilmer went on the road to Emory Rains where, yet again, it dominated its opponent, this time by the score of 63-27.

It could have been worse, except the Buckeye staff had the wherewithal to get its starters out of the game early because they had too much at stake for the playoffs.

"I remember Rains didn't have anything to lose," added Lynch. "Some of them were trying to hurt our players and play dirty. Me and Kris didn't even play defense."

Gilmer finished the year 10-0 and won the district championship. For Traylor, it was his twelfth district championship in 15 years at the helm. An amazing feat for such a competitive region.

He and his staff had also accomplished another remarkable feat. Their regular season point total was 613, only 25 points behind the '75 Big Sandy Wildcats mark at the same point in the year. The Buckeyes' number also sat behind only six other teams in the history of Texas high school football across all classifications. Not bad for a team that usually took out its starters by halftime.

It was playoff time now, and Gilmer wasn't planning on having its timecard expire any time before mid-December in Arlington.

Texarkana's Pleasant Grove was Gilmer's first test, and the Hawks just so happened to be Traylor's first playoff nemesis as a head coach. He'd lost to them 10-0 back in 2001.

But both programs were at very different stages now. Gilmer was competing for its third state title in 15 years under the same head coach, and Pleasant Grove was in year one under first-time head coach Josh Gibson.

Gibson was hired from Frisco High School, where he spent the last nine years serving under his father, Vance. The young, passionate coach saw Pleasant Grove as a diamond in the rough and was attempting to do what his first-round counterpart had so long ago. But this game was all about the Buckeyes. And, really, all about McLane Carter.

The senior quarterback lit up the Hawks defense connecting on 8 of 10 passes for 194 yards and three touchdowns. As had been the practice, he and the other starters did all their work in the first half, and Gilmer cruised to a 50-7 opening round win.

Carter was playing his best ball of the year, and he followed up his first round showing with another masterful performance, this time against Waco Connally; the senior passed for 280 yards and four touchdown passes on 15 of 20 attempts. All his teammates got in on the scoring act and Gilmer swept Connally with an 80-21 beatdown.

Carter was operating at such a high level that even his own coaches were amazed.

"The kid can spin the ball," said Jeff Traylor. "He's a great leader. A competitor."

He was also on pace to match his older brother G.J.'s marks for yards and touchdowns in a single season, a feat that most would have scoffed at only a few years back.

"I still remember when Coach Traylor came up to me when I was a kid and said, 'McLane, you're going to do something that G.J. never did.' I was like, 'What did my brother not do?' He said, 'You're going to win a state championship.'"

Former Gilmer quarterback G.J. Kinne sits next to his younger brother, McLane Carter, on signing day. Carter is also joined by his quarterbacks coach, Alan Metzel, and head coach Jeff Traylor. Carter idolized his older brother, but eventually did something that even his brother never did: win a state championship. (Courtesy of Jeff Traylor)

Traylor accepts the 2009 state championship trophy from UIL Executive Director, Dr. Charles Breithaupt, at midfield of SMU's stadium after Gilmer's 43-26 victory over Abilene Wylie. To Traylor's left, clapping his hands, is quarterback Darian "Stump" Godfrey. (*Gilmer Mirror*/Mary Laschinger Kirby)

"I believe that all of us want to be cared for, we all want to be valued. If you can make someone better at what they love to do and care for them, there's nothing they won't do for you."
--Jeff Traylor

Chapter 12: Championship Culture

The Buckeyes' trajectory of success would have been a pipedream when Jeff Traylor took over the program. But from the start his vision was clear, to raise up both the school district and the town of Gilmer—and to create a championship culture. And he succeeded beyond all odds.

The culture—Traylor's culture—rested on four pillars: discipline and accountability of the coaches and players, the best coaching ensemble across the state, a deeply Christian commitment to the program with a true brotherhood among the coaches, and a do-or-die competitiveness.

"The school started taking pride, and the community started taking pride, when we began winning, in about 2004," said Kurt Traylor. "It didn't happen all of a sudden. It took us four years to build a championship football team and another eight to ten years to turn around the girls' sports program."

"I still remember Jeff saying he used to tell people early in his tenure that if the school gets better, property values go up, and businesses are better," said Kerry Lane. "He said we can start it with this football program, and he was right. And then most importantly, the team won, and he delivered."

"There's a sense of pride that comes with winning," said Stacy Crews.

Crews had been hired by Jeff as the coordinator of girls sports in 2012, and, under her guidance, the girls teams became statewide competitors in track, volleyball and basketball.

"Once the community realized that sports play a big role in kids wanting to be at school, they rallied around us, doing things like painting Go Buckeyes murals on their windows. You didn't see that before Jeff," she said.

"Before Jeff and Albritton came along, there was kind of a resentment. The administration had put all of this money into the school, and the teams weren't winning games. Then Albritton comes along with Jeff and his staff. They realized that winning at sports would carry over into making a difference academically, and they did everything they could to attract kids to the sports programs."

Jeff was an equalizer who raised the Buckeyes to excellence. And he was an equalizer in the tricky dynamics between the town's haves and have-nots.

"I remember talking with Jeff, and him saying that what we do out here will change our school, change our town," said Kerry Lane. "Being from the area and understanding the nuances of the community, Jeff was able to get both populations—those with money and those without it—to be involved, and that meant everyone. You were going to have Mr. Southwell cooking sausage and eggs every Friday morning, and all of these older men treated the guys like they're their grandsons."

Academics as well as athletics soared during Jeff's tenure.

"This school system and community have always been considered 'country,'" said Gilmer superintendent and Traylor supporter Rick Albritton. "We're about eighty-five percent economically disadvantaged. The poverty is generational.

Many people work multiple jobs. They want something to believe in. The football team gave them something to believe in."

"We have the second most academic distinctions of any high school in the state of Texas," said Gilmer principal Brian Bowman. "We're now in the top three percent of Texas, and we're tied for the most in East Texas. Our band continues to get a Division I rating, our theater department advances deep in competitions, and our FFA is the third largest in the entire state regardless of our classification."

***

When it came to assembling the best staff, Traylor believed in continuity. Besides the occasional pick up here and there to bring in new ideas and different perspectives, the Gilmer staff was full of mainstays.

"I swear Traylor had a small college staff coaching 3A ball," said Pat McCown. "They come earlier and stayed later, and they're just smarter. Their kids don't make mistakes. They're drilled. When you have a staff that's so good that you can bring in guys like that Longview coach who went to the 5A state championship to just coach a position for you, then you're pretty good."

"Continuity is such a big part of it," said Matt Turner. "I learned that from the Nebraska Cornhuskers. They had such continuity. When they finally got rid of Solich, some of those people had been there twenty-plus years. That never happens. I always saw that as the model and the key to success. You get good people, and you try to keep them."

Traylor's core cast that became the culture keepers for Gilmer football were Alan Metzel, Todd Barr, Kurt Traylor, and Matt Turner. They grew into a band of brothers, each one bringing their own unique strengths to the family, working together as a team.

Alan Metzel brought counsel and wisdom. Todd Bar brought intelligence and stability. Kurt Traylor brought pride and toughness. Matt Turner brought professionalism and mentoring.

"He's (Jeff) the best at managing people and coaches," said Kerry Lane. "He knew how to create an environment that thrived on competition. Everybody wanted to be the guy that gave Jeff advice."

Traylor was also incredible with staff retention. He knew how talented his staff was, and he kept them on board, even though other schools wooed them with head coaching jobs.

"We had several people who looked around and even interviewed at places," said Metzel. "But Jeff made an environment where you liked working here. You were going to have success. You were going to have access. He did a great job of continuing to make it worth your while financially and with our teaching schedules. He made sure that we weren't overloaded and that we could have the coaching careers that we dreamed of. It wasn't worth it to move to another school."

Traylor was adamant that his staff have the highest pay in East Texas, and he had that leeway because he was backed by Rick Albritton, who knew how important continuity was to the Buckeyes' success.

"I have three beliefs about coaching," said Traylor. "First, I believe people want to be respected, and they want to be given a job with responsibility and accountability; second, they want to be paid well; and third, they wanted to know that the time they were putting into coaching at Gilmer wasn't wasted."

The staff had all three, and that earned their loyalty.

"I also believe that all of us want to be cared for, we all want to be valued. If you can make someone better at what they love to do and care for them, there's nothing they won't do for you," Traylor said.

The school district's investment in the continuity of Traylor and his coaching staff had created an organism that was built for the long haul. After 10 years together, a system was fully in place that ensured clarity of roles; helped make future decisions; and fought against complacency.

Traylor was a stickler for detail and organization. He studied the coach's Bible, *Finding the Winning Edge,* by three-time Super Bowl winner Coach Bill Walsh, who outlined the basic organizational, coaching and system philosophies that the staff used to guide their processes.

"From the standpoint of details and organization, from who is driving the bus Week Six to JV uniforms put up on Friday morning of Week Nine, we want every staff member clearly informed. It takes a lot of time, but it helps," said Metzel.

To implement his strategies, Jeff looked for smart coaches who loved kids and were willing to learn. Character was critical, too.

If coaches had those basic attributes, "Jeff didn't care about the rest. We believe we can teach you how to be a good coach," Metzel said.

Traylor, too, was willing to learn. He was a good listener.

"He has such a strong personality, but he really listens. If you say something good, the next day it's implemented," said Metzel.

He listened not only to his staff but also to parents and their concerns.

"Parents would come up and gripe, but he still listened and saw if there's something here that we need to get better at. It made the program better, and it never became stagnant," Metzel said.

"Jeff realized that success could be your worst enemy, that you could get lax. We recognized that and we fought it—and the willingness to change and try new things was key to that."

Traylor also built a championship culture on his Christian beliefs. The staff did their utmost at their jobs to glorify God.

"When I hire people, they don't work for me. They work for God," Traylor said. "I don't have to monitor them like you do other employees because they're working for a higher being."

Coleman felt that spirit every day he went to the fieldhouse, "surrounded by people who are going to do everything in their power to do the best for the kids. It helped us all be competitive in the best possible way because we didn't want to let the players down, and they didn't want to let us or each other down."

Barr summed the atmosphere up in two simple sentences: "We were like brothers. And we loved doing what we do."

The level of accountability the coaching staff demanded from one another and from their players also became a trademark of their championship culture.

"We always talk about how the kids you coach are a reflection of you," said Kurt. "If you coach them to be tough, they're going to be tough. If you coach them to be soft asses, they're going to be soft asses. But if the kids are going to put the work in, the coaches need to put the work in, too."

"It was very much a college atmosphere. You had your own room. You had autonomy, but you better get it done right—that was the attitude," said Kerry Lane. "Whatever coaching position you had, let's say inside receivers, you were responsible for their grades, assignments, and their being on time to meetings."

Traylor demanded loyalty as well as accountability.

"If you have a best friend that coaches at Gladewater, then you don't tell them what we do. If you have another coach that wants to pick your brain, we don't do that. It was us against the world, but Jeff loved that," said Lane.

"It was shocking, because Jeff is such a people person," added Lane. "But don't ever get it twisted. When it came to football, we were going to lock the doors of the fieldhouse, and it was us thirteen coaches against everybody else in the world, and we were going to beat everyone's ass. No one came into our circle. We didn't discuss even the plays of a game with opposing coaches. We didn't hang out with them at the track or socialize with them in big groups."

The members abided by this nearly sacred loyalty.

"We were very loyal to each other," said Jeff. "We always said all wrong is all right as long as we're all. I'd challenge anyone to find any of our assistants or me to ever bad mouth any of our coaches. I think we'd all die before we would take each other down."

"We're a family," said Kurt. "We're going to keep it as a family. The reason we were successful is because we were going to keep it in house."

"We have this group, and everything that happens within this group, even when new guys are hired, they are from the group," added Keith Tate. "Loyalty was and is the highest priority."

Gilmer's championship culture was also a family-oriented culture where the coaches' kids were a priority.

"I remember one time my wife called and was freaking out because our son had gotten stung by a scorpion, and she didn't know what to do," said Lane. "I told her, 'Relax, it's an East Texas scorpion. It's like a bee sting.' I hung up the phone, and Traylor and Turner both look at me and said, 'Get your stuff and go home.' It was that kind of environment."

But success and growth weren't always smooth for the young, brash coach. The machine Traylor had created and the internal pressures he put on himself could take their toll.

"Coaches Outreach started around that time, and the first one I ever went to I got dizzy and had to go outside of the hotel, which was in Hot Springs," said Traylor. "I passed out, hit my head, and busted it up. Ended up having to go to the hospital."

"I'll never forget Tommy (Maxwell), the head of Coaches Outreach, came to the hospital with me. When we got in the back room, he said, 'Let me guess. I'll bet you teach Sunday School, and you're probably a deacon. I'll bet you're the AD and the head football coach, probably call the plays, probably a husband and father—and like most coaches you never tell anybody "No."'"

"'Son, you're exhausted, and you can't do it by yourself. You're going to burn out, and you're not going to live to see your kids if you don't change.'"

"He was the first person that ever kind of told me that it was okay to say 'No,'" said Traylor.

But easing off the accelerator was easier said than done.

***

After the 2004 season and their first state championship, the Buckeyes found themselves with a target on their backs. Gilmer wasn't seen as an underdog or emerging program anymore. They had the eyes of East Texas on them.

The following season began with very few setbacks. Again, the Buckeyes captured a district title, its fourth in a row, and finished the regular season with only one blemish at 9-1. After avenging its lone regular season loss to Daingerfield by a convincing score of 42-32, the Buckeyes were then set up for an exciting second round match against the Canton Eagles.

Canton, led by the star quarterback and head coach's son, G.J. Kinne, had just captured its first district championship in 25 years. All signs pointed to a points battle where it would come down to whose defense could slow down the other's offense. Unfortunately, Gilmer came out on the wrong end.

After managing to put up an impressive 58 points, its highest point total of the year, the Buckeyes came up three points short. Kinne threw for 430 yards, and the Eagles put up 61 points to get the playoff win.

"We had a lot more talent than them, too, but we were undisciplined," said Traylor. "We still weren't ready. It was almost like we had done it (won a state championship) and that was enough. I wanted it to be if we didn't win a state championship, it was a failure."

Unfortunately, one of his most trying seasons as a head coach was coming up, and it would involve the team that had just defeated him.

In April of 2005 word quickly spread about Canton head football coach, Gary Joe Kinne, being shot by a disgruntled parent. The horrific incident made national headlines, and the family had experienced a level of trauma that few had ever known, especially his son, G.J.

A former player at Baylor, Coach Kinne had accepted an offer to rejoin his alma mater as an assistant coach under Guy Morris after miraculously coming back to lead Canton to its best season in 25 years. His son, G.J., was the reigning 3A Offensive Player of the Year and still had his senior year to play. After the community continued to be split on the incident from 2005, G.J.'s mom decided that him and his younger brother needed to find a safe landing place for his final year, a community where both brothers would thrive.

The place the family chose to resettle was Gilmer. But the move wasn't a smooth one.

In East Texas, Gilmer had become the team to beat—and to hate. Kinne's transferring in only added fuel to the fire because it was perceived that Jeff had moved in on G.J. and recruited him for the Buckeyes. UIL rules don't allow for public schools to recruit other athletes to their teams, so the move was seen by critics as a clear violation.

"I got killed by other coaches on that one," said Traylor. "By haters. It is what it is. The truth was that Gilmer didn't have to recruit. When you win, when you have facilities, and kids get athletic scholarships to top college programs, the families come to you. But people love to talk."

The accusation went all the way to the UIL after the districts' superintendents voted 2-2 on whether Kinne should be allowed to play. The UIL eventually sided with Gilmer. It ruled that all procedures had checked off, and the Buckeye staff had done nothing wrong.

While that part was stressful, Kinne's regular season production was pure joy. The Buckeyes cruised to a 10-0 regular season while averaging over 55 points a game. Kinne would go on to capture his second 3A Offensive Player of the Year award, and another state championship seemed completely doable for Gilmer.

"We were loaded," said Alan Metzel.

The Buckeyes had all of the talent in the world, but there was something off, and the head coach bore the brunt of the criticism. The internal pressure and external flack were the most Traylor had ever encountered.

The 2006 season started to feel like a powder keg.

Liberty-Eylau's LaMichael James, an Oregon commit, was just the spark to ignite it.

"We ended up turning it over three times in the second half against Liberty-Eylau," said Traylor. "The momentum got going, and the crowd was against us. Officials were against us. It was the perfect storm."

Liberty-Eylau, which didn't even win its own district, shocked the region and the rest of the state with its first round upset of Gilmer by a score of 39-36. The Leopards from Texarkana weren't shocked, though. They had a future NFL running back in James and ended up riding the momentum all the way to a 3A state championship.

Traylor was devastated. He knew the level of talent he had that year. He also knew they were "off" as a program. It was time to get back to the ethos that made him and his staff so special.

"I realized I had become too much of a player's coach," said Traylor. "I had to distance myself some. I was so close to them along the way that I became too attached, and I couldn't make the right decisions. So, I hired a lot of former players that I really respected, and I let them get in the trenches more with the players. That's when I truly started functioning more as a *head* coach."

In addition to hiring some of his former players, Traylor brought back one of his closest mentors who had been a key part of the Marshall-Jacksonville regimes. He needed to re-center, and he wanted to do it surrounded by the coaches he knew and trusted the most.

"Wayne Coleman was a big hire in 2007," added Traylor.

Coleman had left Danny, Matt, Jeff, and the Jacksonville Indians back in 1997 to take the head job at Beeville. After turning the Beeville program into a winner, he then took the head job at Fort Worth Brewer for four years followed by one year at Trinity.

"Jeff and I were talking on the phone, complaining about things we wanted to see fixed in our programs, and he asked if I wanted to come to Gilmer," said Coleman. "I thought about it, and then I went and told my wife, 'Hey, we're moving to Gilmer.'"

Coleman had always been an offensive coach, but Traylor knew Coleman's intelligence translated well to other areas, too. He needed a gifted coach to take over the secondary; and the first thing he wanted his new hire to do was watch the previous season's loss to Liberty-Eylau.

"So, Jeff has me watching the game on film of when they lost. Todd Barr comes in and asks me what I think. I told him straight off that this player shouldn't even have been on the field, and Todd told me that the kid was all he had, which I found amazing because Gilmer was number one in the state. I told him, 'Coach, there's no way that kid could tackle LaMichael James in a phone booth. He wouldn't touch him. Please tell me he's graduating,' and he was."

Coleman wanted the Buckeyes to get more athletic on the field and put speed on defense.

"You're exactly what I've been needing," Barr told him. "I need someone to tell when I'm wrong."

"I guess that's why Jeff brought me here," Coleman said. "So don't worry, I'll give my opinion."

***

The old nucleus was back together, and one of the staff's smartest decisions after Coleman came on was naming Darian "Stump" Godfrey the starting quarterback for the 2007 season. The sophomore had one of the greatest names in Texas high school football, and he was about to put the program back on the right track. At the conclusion of his first season at quarterback, Gilmer was back in the state championship game, where the final contest was to be played in Baylor's Floyd Casey Stadium.

"We had Cowboys Stadium secured," said Traylor, "but we ended up losing the coin toss to Liberty Hill so we played at Baylor—and, to make matters worse, Stump had a broken thumb."

Another challenge for the Buckeyes was the weather in Waco that day. It was cold and windy, perfect for Liberty Hill's run-oriented offense but bad for Gilmer's passing attack.

Liberty Hill ended up rolling to a 38-13 victory behind their trademark Slot-T offense.

"I knew they were that good," said Traylor. "I think our defense did all they could do, but we needed to score with them, and we just couldn't."

The following year (2008), Gilmer captured its eighth straight district title. In the fourth round of the playoffs, they eventually bowed out to an upstart Carthage Bulldog program, now revitalized by second-year head coach Scott Surratt.

"We had the ball on the last drive, and Stump ended up throwing an interception," said Traylor. "It was a shootout, and Scott was loaded. That year started a pretty unbelievable three-year run for them."

Carthage went on to win the game 31-28 and won its next two games to capture its first of three straight 3A state championships.

The Buckeyes had lost to the eventual state champion the last three seasons, and two of them by narrow defeats. Almost the entire team was coming back for the 2009 season, led by senior quarterback Stump Godfrey. Going into the offseason, the team had laser-like focus.

But Traylor's attention was briefly diverted.

He'd been at his alma mater for nine years now. During this time, Gilmer had played in two state championships, won one, and captured eight district titles in a row. It was a remarkable feat that caught the attention of interested suitors.

Coppell was one suitor that Traylor took seriously. The district presented the opportunity to coach at a 5A school, which was the highest level at the time, and earn significantly more money.

"Everything was perfect at Coppell. They did a great job. The administration did everything they could do to get me there. They even called my wife, Cari. Next thing I knew, we were down there looking."

"I remember walking through it," said Cari Traylor. "I went down there with him for an interview because they interviewed me, too. He was literally so back and forth in his mind about what he should do."

In the midst of privately going through the interview process, Jeff's star quarterback—unaware of his coach's turmoil—offered him a promise one day in spring training.

"That offseason, Stump promised me he'd win me another championship—so I decided to stay," he said.

Godfrey's words could be taken to heart because of his leadership ability. He was playing on a different level, and everyone in the program knew it, especially his head coach.

"Darian's athleticism is unquestionable," added Traylor. "It's the other intangibles that made him a great player, like his tremendous leadership skills."

"On every state championship team, we'd had a quarterback who was not going to let us lose," said Kurt Traylor. "Stump was not going to let us get beat. Was not. He knew the work he put in was going to make us successful, and he trusted us coaches."

Traylor and his program were now firing on all cylinders, and he was at peace with his decision to remain in Gilmer. The staff was fully aligned and loaded with the best coaching ensemble across the state, and the team was experienced and rich with talent. Traylor even picked up another star coach prior to the season, Tim Russell, a close friend of Alan Metzel, who had just finished his tenure as head coach at Pine Tree.

When the fall finally rolled around, the Buckeyes dashed out to another undefeated regular season, Traylor's fifth in 10 years, and captured Gilmer's ninth straight district championship. They cruised through their first two playoff opponents, before edging out a tough Navasota team in the third round. This put the Buckeyes in the semifinals against the tradition-rich Cuero Gobblers.

Cuero was making its fifth trip to the semifinals in six years and boasting an undefeated record. The winner of this contest—played at Sam Houston State's Bowers Stadium in

Huntsville—was predicated to be the state champion by East Texas football fans.

After dashing out to a 20-7 Cuero lead, Gilmer fought back led by none other than Stump Godfrey.

Godfrey accounted for five touchdowns on the ground and another in the air. He proved why he would eventually be named the 3A Player of the Year. But Cuero wouldn't back down.

"The lead ended up changing seven times," said Traylor. "They took the lead, then we'd take the lead. It was an awesome game."

Clinging to a six-point lead, Gilmer forced one final turnover on downs and won the game by a score of 42-36.

"Cuero had a hell of a team, too," said Traylor.

The final game, played at SMU's Ford Stadium, pitted Gilmer against Abilene Wylie. As had been predicted the previous week, the Gilmer-Cuero victor was just too much for Wylie as the Buckeyes overwhelmed them by a score of 43-26.

"We were just way better than Abilene Wylie," added Traylor. "Their coach is awesome. We just had more talent."

With their usual continuity, Traylor and his staff had now delivered two state championships in 10 years. In a town that often gets overlooked, even in East Texas, its football program had exemplified excellence.

In the offseason of 2010, Tim Russell left to take over the head coaching position at the place he first began, Harmony High School.

In true Traylor fashion, when he lost one star staffer, he picked up another in Robert Bero, the former head coach of the Longview Lobos. Bero coached the Lobos from 1988-1999, and his 1997 state finalist team remains one of the most talked about rosters to ever grace East Texas. That team ended up getting beaten in the finals by Mike Johnston's Katy Tigers, and the Lobos never could get back to the finals under Bero's tenure; a state title ring was the only thing missing for the old ball coach.

By their second state championship, Traylor's band of brothers had been in place long enough to start guiding the next generation of Buckeye families they had already coached, and even began coaching their own sons.

Together, the coaches and the community helped turn around an economically disadvantaged farming town, even raising property values. Gilmer ISD had become a very different place than the school the Traylor boys remembered attending.

Jeff and Cari Traylor celebrate after Gilmer's first state championship win in 2004 that took place at their alma mater, Stephen F. Austin State University. Now approaching the 2014 state championship game, they had raised their family in Gilmer for 15 years. (Courtesy of Cari Traylor)

Blake Lynch (#9), Kris Boyd (#21), Chase Tate (#25), and McLane Carter (#4) represent the Gilmer Buckeyes at midfield of "Jerry World" for the coin toss prior to their state championship game against West Orange-Stark. (Courtesy of Ruel Felipe)

"We're going to come back and beat this team for Dez."
--Jeff Traylor

Chapter 13: Jerry World

After two effortless playoff wins, Gilmer and Gladewater gave East Texas the playoff game—the day after Thanksgiving—that it deserved, when Kris Boyd scored a go-ahead touchdown with under a minute to play to give the Buckeyes the win. In Longview's Lobo Stadium with a full crowd, fans were able to witness what was arguably the greatest high school football game ever played in East Texas.

"I didn't think there would ever be a game that would surpass the game at Sam Houston versus Cuero in '09. But there was one and it was that Gilmer versus Gladewater game, maybe the best I've ever seen," said Keith Tate.

The team had always felt that this year was different, and that feeling was now intensified.

"We expected to win," said Todd Barr. "We had the kids. Our community had expectations. From the get-go, we knew if we could stay healthy and have some luck, this could be a pretty special season."

The Buckeyes had also successfully made it to the sweet spot of the season where player engagement was natural. At this point, there were only potentially three games left for them, and, for some players, that meant only three more games left in their Buckeye careers. Pettiness over playing time or complaining about the degree of difficulty was gone. Everyone was poised to get the team its third championship, and they'd do whatever it took to get there.

"Football is not easy to play," said Kerry Lane. "It's hot, and you put a helmet on your head, and then run around and throw your body into another body. It hurts. It's not natural. It's a hard sport to play. When motivation runs low, they play because they love their teammates."

"Sure, Kris Boyd was easy to motivate, because he was headed straight to a top college program, and he wound up playing in the NFL. Jeff used to always say, 'How do you motivate the backups?' They get to be a part of a great team, a brotherhood."

The 2014 roster had bought in, and their next opponent was about to face their determination.

Back at Lobo Stadium for the second week in a row, Gilmer faced off in the quarterfinals against East Texas powerhouse, Atlanta. The Rabbits came in with a 12-1 record and a defensive game plan designed to limit the Buckeyes' air attack.

"Coach Traylor kept mentioning beforehand how much speed they had," said McLane Carter. "He just kept emphasizing speed, speed, speed to us. Kris Boyd and Blake Lynch weren't having that though."

Together, Boyd and Lynch made four offensive touchdowns on game night, and Carter again showed why he had become one of the best quarterbacks in the state. Going 15-19 for 239 yards and three touchdowns, even his lone mistake turned into a Gilmer score when he tossed his second interception of the year late in the first half, and then Lynch stripped the ball and scored from 22 yards out.

"Once we get rolling, we're real hard to stop," said Lynch. "If we get a rhythm going, we're going to put up a lot of points."

By halftime, Gilmer was winning 50-12. The level of detail and commitment to excellence the players showed following such an emotional game against rival Gladewater floored their head coach.

"That's the thing people miss," added Traylor. "Fans love play-calls, fans love chatter; but it's about effort, it's about trust, it's about love. I know that stuff sounds corny but that's what we're really about."

The final score read 64-25, and the Buckeyes were one win away from playing for a state championship. Waiting for them was a perennial power in Celina.

The Celina Bobcats had won more state championships than any other school in Texas regardless of classification. Built by legendary coach G.A. Moore, the program won six state titles under his reign before he passed it off to his long-time defensive coordinator Butch Ford.

Ford captured two more state titles as head coach, which gave the program eight total, just ahead of Katy, and tied for the lead with Southlake Carroll.

In 2012, Ford retired, and handed it over to another Celina assistant, his offensive coordinator, Bill Elliott. Elliott had been a former player at TCU who was ready to put his stamp on Bobcat football. After two solid years under his direction, Celina's 2014 team was back in true form, playing big games that caught the attention statewide as the winningest program in Texas.

The previous week, Celina had won a hard-fought game against Sweetwater, an opponent that came into the contest undefeated thanks to a high-caliber offense. Elliott thought the previous week had been the perfect preparation for Gilmer. He vastly underestimated the pleasure that gritty East Texas teams take in trouncing blue blood programs like his.

Elliott made the mistake of sharing his take on the game with the media.

"You look at the skill-kids that Sweetwater had, and the ones Gilmer has, and there's not a lot of difference," said Elliott to *ETFinalScore.com*. "When you run a 4.4, you run a 4.4."

Always the master motivator, Traylor put the thorn of Elliot's words into the side of the Buckeyes.

"Coach Traylor knew that comment would rile us up," said Lynch.

He recalled Traylor's pregame speech, one that struck at the core of his players.

"Coach told us, 'These guys are not like you. They drive Mercedes. They grew up with pools in their backyards. They don't respect y'all.'"

The message was jet fuel on Gilmer's fire.

In the first 6:50 of the game, Gilmer scored 26 points. Six different players went on to score touchdowns, and Carter had six of his nine passing completions result in scores. Blake Lynch had five touchdowns himself. Traylor didn't even have to put Carter in for the second half. It was clear to everyone watching that Celina was being owned.

When the final seconds ticked off the clock, the score read Gilmer 67, Celina 14. The Buckeyes were headed back to the state championship.

"I remember the fans were crazy, but I also remember the opposing players coming up and congratulating us," said Lynch. "Most schools are emotional and mad after a loss, but I just remember they were so respectful. Their coaches were respectful. We even all circled up at the end and prayed."

***

In 2010, the UIL entered an agreement with Dallas Cowboys owner Jerry Jones to hold its 3A-5A state championship games in the Cowboys' brand-new stadium, located in Arlington. It quickly became the most sought-after venue in the country after it opened in May 2009 and was dubbed "Jerry World."

Boasting the largest HDTV video display board directly above the field, it was as Texas-big, flashy, and spectacular as you'd expect in the Lone Star State. Jerry's World would go on to host Super Bowl XLV in 2011 and be chosen as the site of college football's first-ever CFP Championship game in 2015.

In a state where high school football was iconic, it only made sense that championship games would be played in Jerry World. Gilmer's first time playing in "the cathedral" was 2012 when it rode an unexpected hot streak before eventually losing to heavily favored Navasota. The next time they wouldn't be the underdog as they played West Orange-Stark on the home turf of the Dallas Cowboys.

"There's nothing like Cowboys Stadium," said Lynch. "You get a whole bunch of country guys from East Texas inside that stadium. It's surreal. It's something that a lot of us only get to do once in our lives."

The Buckeyes may not have been the underdog, but they also weren't shoe-ins. It was going to be a heavyweight match with two tradition-rich programs that represented blue-collar communities battling it out on the turf.

In the 15 years since Traylor had taken over, Gilmer had won 12 district titles while West Orange-Stark had won 11. Since Cornel Thompson had taken over the Mustang program in 2011, both teams had advanced to at least the third round of the playoffs every single year. Most importantly, both programs already had two state titles in their trophy cases and badly wanted a third.

***

Orange is in the southeastern part of the state, a region of refineries and humidity. Along with Beaumont and Port Arthur, it comprises the "Golden Triangle," so called because of the wealth that flowed in from the Spindletop oil boom in 1901. Eighty years later, this once thriving Southeast Texas area began to fall on hard times, when its refineries and petrochemical plants began laying off employees, many of them blue-collar workers. By the 1980s, Orange and neighboring Port Arthur faded into shadows of their former selves, as gritty as East Texas but never to be confused with that stand-alone region, although both occupy the eastern part of the state.

But like East Texas, the Golden Triangle is a hotbed for football talent. In 1971, Beaumont Mayor Ken Ritter declared the region to be the football capital of the world, because so many of its hometown boys went into Division I programs and then the NFL. In fact, *Dave Campbell's Texas Football* magazine publishes an annual breakdown of where the majority of native Texans playing Division I college football players come from and the Golden Triangle region is always at or near the top.

Even within the Golden Triangle, the West Orange-Stark Mustangs stood out for their talent and were the pride of the region, especially after the town was nearly leveled by Hurricane Rita in 2005 and Hurricane Ike in 2008. In a time of continual hardship, the one thing the community could still depend on was Mustang football. The program was shepherded by Dan Ray Hooks for 30 years before he turned it over to long-time assistant Cornel Thompson. Under these great coaches, Stark won back-to-back 4A state titles in the 1980s, and maintained an enviable level of consistency in the 1990s and the 2000's, producing NFL stars like Kevin Smith and Earl Thomas.

This 2014 team was loaded and young, and Thompson knew it would be the biggest test of the year, as did the Buckeye staff.

"Overall, and athletically, they had the most talent of anyone we played that year," said Todd Barr.

The Stangs had Deionte Thompson at safety. The community believed he was the next great secondary player from Stark, every bit as talented as Kevin Smith and Earl Thomas. Alabama head coach Nick Saban thought so as well and made sure to secure a commitment from Thompson over the likes of Texas, Texas A&M, and LSU.

"They had some dogs on their team," said McLane Carter. "I think their whole secondary was DI. They were bigger and stronger than us. But we were faster."

"I mean, they had Deionte," said Lynch. "We knew it was going to be a fight."

A chartered bus departed Gilmer for Arlington on December 18th, one day before the game, but there was one stop they had to make as a team before they were on the road.

"We went out to Dez's gravesite," said Kurt Traylor. "The headstone was there, and we got out as a team and took a picture there. We all felt he was the reason we made it this far, so it was important that we honored him. He wasn't going to be on the field, but he was, if you know what I mean."

"We all got to just reminisce together," added Blake Lynch. "Talked about what he would've done to play for state. It was a super emotional experience."

When the team finally arrived in Arlington, they returned to their usual disciplined routine. But even under the pressure of playing in the most important game of the season, Traylor made sure the players had fun.

Once the official meetings were finished in the designated team room the evening before the game, Traylor told everyone to stay put, and a couple of the younger coaches started taking turns doing impressions of some of the older coaches to lighten up the mood.

"They were doing Metzel, Turner, and Traylor," said Lynch. "It's something that I'll remember for the rest of my life for sure. They got Turner the best. Coach Bay was the one who did it. We were dying laughing."

Afterward, Traylor dismissed the team to their rooms for a good night's sleep so they'd be ready for peak performance—and soon after, quarterbacks McLane Carter and Blake Lynch started feeling bad.

"It turned out to be strep throat, but we didn't know what was wrong, so Coach Lane went and got us some flu medicine that night. We felt terrible," said Lynch.

The next morning, "We woke up and we're like it doesn't matter," said Lynch. "We have to go out and win this game."

The moment was finally here.

The Stangs drew first blood when they scored on a 12-yard run late in the first quarter. Gilmer was unable to make anything happen on offense, and the Stangs followed up with two more touchdowns by Stark in the second, this time through the air. The score was 19-0 with 4:52 left in the first half, and Gilmer was getting manhandled for the first time all year.

"We just couldn't get anything going," said Lynch.

"They were spanking us," said Carter. "They were running Cover 2, and I'd never seen that before. They were covering ground on us. I just couldn't find a rhythm. I had never played football like that. They were hitting me, and I felt like I didn't know what the heck was going on."

The Buckeye offense did manage to respond on the next possession and finished a quick drive off with a Kris Boyd touchdown run.

If Gilmer could go in at the half down only two touchdowns, that would've been a positive. But the Mustangs answered again scoring their fourth touchdown of the half with 24 seconds left to go.

Then, disaster almost struck. After quickly getting the ball into a field position that allowed Gilmer's kicker to try a deep field goal before the half, the kick fell short of the goal posts into the end zone. Anticipating a short kick, Stark put their best player, Deionte Thompson, back in the end zone to catch the ball if it was playable. It fell short, and Thompson gave the crowd a glimpse of just how special he was.

"He returned it 106 yards to the house," said Carter. "Thankfully, it got called back for a penalty. We could've been down 32-7."

The score sat at 25-7 as both teams left the field and headed to their locker rooms. Gilmer was in trouble. They had been dominated on both sides of the ball, and there didn't seem to be any evidence that the second half would be any different.

But in a championship culture, the players and staff thrive on do-or-die challenges.

"Strategy is important but it's your culture that determines whether or not you'll be successful," said Kurt. "Culture is why great organizations sustain success. It drives our expectations and beliefs. Our expectations and beliefs drive our behaviors. And behaviors drive habits. Habits create the future."

Jeff Traylor knew what he had to communicate to his team.

"You know what, I'm not going to say anything. Because you know what, Dez wouldn't allow this. Dez wouldn't want this. Dez would come out and compete."

Traylor grabbed Dez's jersey and held it up. "*This* is why we do this. We're going to come back and beat this team for Dez."

"Jeff's confidence was just so contagious," said Carter. "I had never seen anyone that confident in my life. It was the look on his face. He told us, 'You watch, something magical is about to happen.' That's what I love about Coach Traylor. That guy don't give up."

"Coach Traylor knew what he was doing," added Kris Boyd. "He always had the blueprint."

"Then Kris Boyd started getting fiery," added Carter. "He starts digging into people. He had never been a real vocal leader, but he was up and yelling like I had never seen him do before. We all started spitting faith in each other and spitting belief in each other."

In the start of the second half, Todd Barr's Black Flag defense provided the initial spark for the Buckeyes. Jackson Sikes picked off a Mustang pass on the Gilmer 25, and then McLane Carter delivered a touchdown strike to Nick Smith to give the Buckeyes 14 points. On the ensuing possession, Demarco Boyd stuck Mustang running back Trey Baldwin behind the line of scrimmage, and Tristain Olivares stripped the ball loose. It rolled into Gilmer's end zone, where Devin Smith quickly pounced on it for another Buckeye score. Just like that the Buckeyes were now down by only four points.

"We gained so much confidence in that third quarter defensively," said Barr.

"We shut them down," added Boyd.

In the fourth quarter, with the game finally in striking distance, the offensive staff orchestrated a 14-play, 70-yard drive that finished with a five-yard Blake Lynch touchdown run. The score gave Gilmer its first lead of the game at 28-25.

"We didn't do anything crazy," said Carter. "We just played good football."

After forcing another Mustang punt, Gilmer's Blake Lynch delivered the final blow. Carter opened the drive by tossing a screen pass to Lynch, which he took 54 yards before pulling up limp.

"I pulled my hamstring," recalled Lynch. "I actually fell on my own. Deionte Thompson was at least 10 yards away!"

The injury didn't slow him down much though. A few plays later, Lynch re-entered the game and delivered the final touchdown, a seven-yard run that gave Gilmer a 35-25 lead with 4:59 remaining in the contest.

The Black Flag defense finished out the game in perfect form and delivered a second half shut out. It was a remarkable comeback.

The final stats by the Buckeyes Big Three reflected their talent. Kris Boyd had 145 total yards and a touchdown; Carter was 14-22 through the air for 245 yards and a touchdown; and the move-in, Blake Lynch, had 117 total yards, two touchdowns, as well as the Offensive MVP honor. An early enrollee at Baylor, Lynch also officially graduated from Gilmer High School that day. Not a bad way to go out.

Taking home the Defensive MVP award was Kris Boyd's younger brother, Demarco, who had five tackles including a sack and pass break-up.

"My little brother had the game of his life," said Kris. "Our playmakers made plays, so we came back and won that thing."

The experience was highly emotional for the entire team, especially Carter. He had lost his brother the year before, and he had honored him the best way he knew how.

"When I took that final knee to end it, I heard him say, 'You did it, bro,'" said Carter. "It was just in my head. It freaked me out. I put my hand over my helmet, and I was in disbelief. It had to be my psyche or however you want to take that. There are things that happen in your life when you feel something from another place, like a little piece of energy or something."

Tears streamed down Jeff Traylor's eyes when he spoke to Fox sideline reporter, Erin Hartigan, after the game.

"My kids just kept believing, and we got it for Dez."

The field and the locker room overflowed with euphoria. The exhaustion that comes with playing a full game didn't seem to matter at all. It was time to celebrate.

"It was hectic, exactly what you would expect," added Carter. "We're all running and jumping around yelling, 'We did it for Desmond! We did it for Desmond!'"

It was also a joyful and reflective time for the staff. The older corps of coaches—Barr, Tate, Metzel, Turner, the Traylor brothers, and Coleman—knew how hard it was to win one, and history had taught them to soak it up and appreciate it for what it was, a blessing. Young coaches like Kerry Lane and Olan Johnson were completely fired up. The experience had confirmed that this kind of culture worked and had made them junkies to want to try and do it again, maybe even on their own. And then there were coaches like Robert Bero, a coach's coach, who had spent 42 years coaching young men in East Texas but had never won a ring. This was icing on the cake of a long and storied career.

When asked what this third championship meant to him, Traylor responded, "It's my greatest one because of Robert Bero, a guy that's coached 42 years. We got him his first championship. My nephews are on the team. My son is on the team. My best friends' kids are on the team. I've got former players on the team. I can't tell you how much this means to me. This is my favorite one."

Gilmer celebrates its third state championship in 15 years by beating West Orange-Stark 35-25, and Kris Boyd (#21) holds up the trophy. (Courtesy of Ruel Felipe)

"A lot of great people really love me. They're the reason I don't want to go, but I feel like I need to go. I just think God wants me to go."
--Jeff Traylor

Chapter 14: #bEASTtexas

On January 26th, 2015, the Gilmer faithful packed its downtown square for the nighttime state championship parade. A month had already passed since the Buckeyes had captured their third state title, beating West Orange-Stark, and the party was far from over.

Serving as Master of Ceremonies for the event was KYKX's Harlen the Sports Guy. After warming the crowd up, he introduced Jeff Traylor.

"I still say he's the best coach in all of East Texas," Harlen said before handing the microphone over to Traylor. The crowd was in a frenzy.

Traylor offered a humorous take on Harlen's glowing compliment.

"Believe it or not, Coach Surratt [from Carthage] and I are very good friends, and we were staying at the same place after the state championship," Traylor said. "He was using my phone, and Harlen sent over a text saying, 'Congratulations to the best coach in the state of Texas.' Surratt said, 'You wait until I see Harlen.'"

"Let's just say I bought the next couple of Cokes for Coach Surratt."

The crowd erupted with laughter. The rivalry with Carthage was real for them, and they were ready to do some gloating.

Then, like a pastor preaching to an overflowing congregation, Traylor quieted the crowd by lifting the curtain on his halftime speech in the game against West Orange-Stark.

The question I get asked the most is what did I say at halftime? I will share some of it, and some of it is behind closed doors.

I told them that the only people who believe we're going to come back from this deficit we're in are the players in this room and all my former players, and there's a few fans who'd agree. Very few.

There were a few that held in there. I'll never forget the feeling coming off the field. You have to remember that we're human too; and we doubt at times. That's when we have to go back to trusting our training. And our training says we're capable of coming back from this hole. So, as I'm running off the field, I remember Bridget Fowler encouraging us with all her heart. She basically represented the 200-300 of y'all that were still believing.

There was this other guy on the left that represented the masses. He was calling me every name in the book. And said that my teams always choke in the big game. His exact quote was, "Y'all are all flash and no cash." That was his exact quote. I almost looked up at him.

When the game was over, I thought of many things, and I thought of all you fans, who were so loyal who had to listen to all of the idiots who were bad-mouthing us. I was thinking about how much fun y'all were having in the fourth quarter saying, "I told you so! I told you so! I told you so!"

The Buckeye crowd, standing in the freezing cold, erupted with laughter and applause.

Wanting to leave the moment with something more than a few laughs and interesting stories, Traylor finished his speech by bragging on his team and offering some of the life lessons they practice on a daily basis that are also applicable for the entire community.

Our secret is just this, we really are a family. I know people say that. But we really are. We fight and we get after each other. But we believe in each other tremendously. And in those moments when everybody thinks we're done, we're never done. And that's because of the belief we have in each other.

We've had a great fifteen-year run. We've been more than blessed. Won so many ball games, saved so many kids' lives. And the winning is important because it's fun. Winning is what makes everybody happy. But what I really want the program to be remembered for is how many kids we saved. I hope you'll look deep into how many kids' lives have been changed. Kids you don't even know about. You know about the stars. I wish you looked deeper into the roster. There's a third of those guys that never play. They never play. All they ever do is play scout team. They're on the bench. And it's hard on mommas. It's hard on coaches. To watch their babies never play. But I want you to see how important it is to belong to something and not quit. And hang in there. And that's just a characteristic in life we've all lost.

I don't want to preach. But it's why families fall apart. It's why churches fall apart. It's why communities fall apart. Something's wrong with this world. And we don't hang in there anymore. And we gotta hang in there together. We could all fight. But at the end of the day, we're all Gilmer Buckeyes. And we should all love each other. And hang in there together. That's what life really is.

The thundering applause from the crowd clearly showed how Traylor had become more than the leader of the town's football team. He and his staff had become the moral leaders of this community.

After thanking the fans, Harlen led the crowd in one last chant. It was the chant that propelled the team and the community to get past one of its most challenging times into one of its most euphoric.

"Fans let's send one up. 'Designate' on three. One, two, three: Designate!!!"

After 100 years of football, Gilmer now had 643 total wins, which gave the Buckeyes the 20th most wins of any team in Texas. The 2014 Gilmer team had laid a strong claim to be the best team to ever come out of East Texas. Its offense had just recorded 950 points for the entire season, which was just above 59 points per game, setting the record for the region and finishing second all-time for Texas high school football, regardless of classification. The only school to one-up them was 5A's Aledo, which had 1,023 points in 2013.

For East Texas historians, the score was even more important in that it eclipsed the 1975 Big Sandy team that scored 824 points. The Wildcats' offensive production was the gold standard for the region, and now there was a new marker for others to try and pass.

The Buckeyes were officially a blue blood program that people across the state recognized for its excellence. Traylor's vision for the program had come to fruition.

Gilmer's ascension tracked with the entire East Texas region's growing reputation for producing some of the best teams and talent for the entire state. College coaches were now making the region a priority, and recruiting battles were about to be at an all-time high for who could deliver the Piney Woods region. The college-coach recruiting contest would soon include Jeff Traylor.

***

When the UIL first began awarding state titles, it took ten years for East Texas to have a champion of its own. The very first state championship game in Texas high school football was played between Houston Heights and Cleburne in 1920. Neither team was able to score on the other, and it is in the record books as a tie. The very next year Bryan, near College Station, defeated Dallas Oak Cliff by a score of 35-13 for the first state championship in Texas high school football history. It wasn't until 1930 that Tyler captured the first state title for the East Texas region by defeating Amarillo 25-13. Seven years later, Longview beat Wichita Falls for its first and only state title by 19-12. Unfortunately, these were the only two titles won by the Piney Woods for the first 30 years of state championships games.

In 1998, the region caught fire. The UIL expanded its number of championship games to ten, two for each of the five classifications in Texas. In the previous 78 years of state championship football, the East Texas region had produced 27 titles. From 1998 to 2014, the region produced 30.

But there were only three champions in the top two classifications: the 2001 Lufkin team (5A), the 2002 Texas High team (4A), and the 2004 Tyler Lee team (5A). The smaller schools were bringing home the trophies. Schools such as Tatum, Liberty-Eylau, Gilmer, Carthage, Daingerfield, Waskom, and Tenaha all won multiple titles during this time period. Seeing how much good championship teams did for their towns, communities started pouring money and other resources into their schools' athletics programs. Coaches were paid higher salaries and no longer had to leave for the Metroplex to advance their careers. Facilities were upgraded with some towns funding indoor practice facilities and video scoreboards.

Success built upon success. More appearances in state championship games also meant more exposure for the players on these teams, slowly but surely gaining the recognition of top college coaches. One catalyst for this recognition was the recruitment of a running back from the city of Palestine named Adrian Peterson. In 2003, Peterson was the best running back to come out of the region since John Tyler High School's Earl Campbell. After a highly publicized recruitment contest between Oklahoma and Texas, Peterson selected the Sooners, and Longhorn fans' hearts were broken. Of course, this was before Mack Brown turned the University of Texas back into a national championship contender.

Four years later, Texas High quarterback Ryan Mallett, mentored by Scott Surratt, was the biggest recruit the area had seen since Peterson. Mallett also chose to go out of state, signing with the University of Michigan. He attended as a freshman; but after Lloyd Carr was fired and Rich Rodriguez was brought in, the quarterback knew he would need to transfer to find a more suitable passing attack. Enter Bobby Petrino and the Arkansas Razorbacks. Petrino groomed Mallett to be the pro caliber passer that he knew he could be, and Mallett led Arkansas to the Sugar Bowl.

Then came Gladewater's Daylon Mack. Weighing around 300 pounds with lightning quick feet, Mack brought an onslaught of attention to the region. After seeing him in his inaugural varsity scrimmage, Gabe Brooks of *Scout.com* wrote, "I knew he would likely become the most-heralded recruit in the East Texas region since Ryan Mallett in the 2007 class." Midway through his sophomore year, Texas A&M became the first to recognize his talent and make an offer. The floodgate soon opened after the Aggies' proclamation, and schools like Texas, Alabama, and LSU quickly offered spots to the phenom as well.

By mid-October of his junior year, Mack had acquired offers from every major program in the country, and by the spring of 2014, East Texas saw an increase of 17 Division I signees (32 total) compared to the previous year. College coaches were flocking to the fertile grounds of towns like Gilmer, Carthage, and Tatum.

"That 2015 recruiting class put this spot on the map," said former *ETSN* writer Justin Wells. "You had Daylon Mack as the number one defensive tackle, Larry Pryor as the number one safety out of Sulphur Springs, and Justin Dunning as the number one athlete in the state of Texas. He went to A&M, Kris Boyd went to Texas, and Blake Lynch went to Baylor. It was loaded."

On Oct. 21, 2013, Mack verbally committed to Texas A&M. It was the biggest commitment of the 2015 class thus far, and it sent shockwaves through the entire state. Texas A&M was a program on the rise, and now, too, were the high school programs in the East Texas region.

In 2013 at a preseason football meeting, sports writers Justin Wells, Gabe Brooks, Damon Sayles, and Clint Buckley were brainstorming ideas about how they could increase the presence of their new venture, the *East Texas Sports Network*. Wells came up with the idea to include a "B" at the beginning of East Texas and use it as a social media hashtag. Sayles countered by saying they should do a lowercase "b" and use all caps for the "EAST" part. The result was a hashtag that every college football recruiter now knows to use when recruiting in East Texas: #bEASTtexas.

"It has to be the most recognizable region name," said Wells. "I just don't see other hashtags being used like this. It's on shirts, walls, camp titles. The kids loved it, too."

***

In July of 2012, Texas A&M embarked on a new era. After enduring conference realignment in the Big 12 and watching its rival, the University of Texas (UT), power play all its conference peers with the launching of its own television network, Texas A&M jumped to the Southeastern Conference (SEC). After UT won its fourth national championship in 2005, the next six national championships came from the SEC. They were the premier football conference in the nation, and it wasn't even close. A&M was under the direction of a new football coach, Kevin Sumlin, who was the first African American head coach in program history. Austin has always been perceived as more forward-thinking than College Station, but the Aggies suddenly looked like the more progressive program. They also bumped up a notch in celebrity with the emergence of another East Texan who the world would soon come to know as "Johnny Football."

Johnny Manziel was born in Tyler, Texas. The son of a wealthy family that owned several businesses in the area, he spent his childhood growing up on the sixteenth hole of Tyler's Hollytree Country Club. While his family was known for their great business prowess, their success was later dwarfed by the defeats in their personal lives.

After agreeing as a family that it was in Johnny's best interest to attend a new school, the Manziels moved down to Kerrville at the start of his seventh-grade year so he could eventually enroll in Tivy High School, a 5A district. Manziel flourished in his new setting, where he graduated as a Parade All-American quarterback, in addition to being named Mr. Football in Texas. He received several offers to play college football, but his 5'11 frame deterred some schools from giving him a chance at quarterback, most notably the University of Texas, his favorite team as a boy.

Their loss was A&M's gain. Manziel signed on to compete for the quarterback job. He redshirted his first year on campus; but after the school decided to fire head coach Mike Sherman and bring in Houston's Kevin Sumlin, the new offensive scheme seemed to favor Manziel. He won the starting job and then went on to win a whole lot more. In 2012 as a redshirt freshman, Johnny Manziel led the Aggies to an 11-2 finish, a regular season win over national champion Alabama in Tuscaloosa, and a Cotton Bowl victory over Oklahoma, earning him the Heisman Trophy. His season was a public relations dream for the university and the football program, in particular. They officially had the "cool factor" in the state, and a status that gave them an edge in recruiting, much to the dismay of Texas fans.

***

Every empire eventually falls. From 2001-2009, the University of Texas, under legendary head coach Mack Brown, had a stretch where it won at least 10 games every season. In 2005, it won its fourth national championship behind the dynamic quarterback play of Vince Young, and in 2009 it looked poised to win number five. Mack Brown and Athletics Director,

DeLoss Dodds, had built the most profitable athletic department in all of college sports. But with a single hit on January 7, 2010, in Pasadena, California, the Longhorns began a long fall from college football supremacy.

After forcing a turnover and capitalizing with a field goal, Texas gambled on its ensuing kickoff to Alabama and decided to do an onside kick. It was a bold move for a national championship game, but it paid off because the Longhorns recovered the kick in Alabama territory. Momentum was on Texas's side, and its starting quarterback, Colt McCoy, ran onto the field infusing confidence into his offensive teammates.

McCoy had had a fairy tale career leading up to this point. He was a small-town kid from West Texas whose father was a Texas high school football coach. After setting state records on the 2A level, he accepted a scholarship to the University of Texas with hopes of taking the reins once Vince Young graduated. He redshirted his first year and had a front row seat to watch Young lead Texas to a national championship in the Rose Bowl. He was in awe of Vince, but fully determined to have his turn duplicating that success. Just four years later, he was a first-team All-American, who had led the Longhorns to an undefeated regular season, a Big 12 championship, and a spot in the Rose Bowl playing the University of Alabama for the national championship.

At the Rose Bowl, the first four plays from scrimmage favored the Longhorns after they recovered the onside kick. Texas was now inside the Alabama ten-yard line with four downs to score. Offensive coordinator, Greg Davis, called for McCoy to run a speed option to the right. It was a play he had run several times throughout the season. McCoy took the snap and rolled right. Alabama decided to take away the running back option, so Colt ended up keeping the ball and trying to make a play. He was met at the line of scrimmage by defensive tackle

Marcel Dareus, and was taken down. The play looked completely normal to everyone in the stadium, but something was off. McCoy arose from the tackle and motioned that he needed to come out. He wasn't feeling any pain though; instead, he couldn't feel anything on his right arm at all. The doctors ruled it a pinched nerve, and McCoy was benched for the rest of the game.

To replace him, coaches sent in Garrett Gilbert, the quarterback of the future for Texas. He was Mr. Football in Texas and had also earned the Gatorade Male Athlete of the Year award after leading Lake Travis to a state championship win over Longview the previous season. Gilbert made a valiant effort, but a Nick Saban-led defense proved to be too much in the end. Alabama was victorious by a score of 37-21. The loss stung. Many thought that Texas was good enough to win, and McCoy was devastated by the timing.

"I was so heartbroken," he later wrote in *The Players' Tribune*. "I just wanted to be out there, fighting with the team. It wasn't supposed to end like this."

There are conflicting reports about what would have happened with the coaching staff if Mack Brown had won its second national championship in 2009. Regardless, the circumstances seemed perfect for a transition of leadership. In 2008, Texas hired the hottest assistant coach in college football, Will Muschamp, away from Auburn. Muschamp served as the defensive coordinator and was anointed Brown's head coach-in-waiting.

It was an innovative move by Dodds and Brown to protect the Longhorns' future since Brown was getting up in age. The *Austin American-Statesman's* Kirk Bohls wrote, "Muschamp's ascension conveys to fans and recruits that Texas values what it has now as one of the elite programs in the country, and wants to maintain. This smart, bold move should bring coaching stability, sustained recruiting, and possibly expanded recruiting into the Southeast and a continued framework for success."

After the 2008 season, they also had the nation's number one quarterback signed in Gilbert. *Scouts Inc.* even predicted that Gilbert would win the Heisman trophy before his senior year at Texas. Long-term success seemed inevitable, but the hit on McCoy changed everything. After failing to win his second national championship, Brown declined to hand over the keys of the empire to Muschamp. He wasn't finished coaching.

The 2010 season started with a depleted team. The offense wasn't performing as it had in the past, and fans grew impatient and critical with Gilbert's development and with offensive coordinator Greg Davis's play calls. Texas finished 5-7 and had its first losing season since 1997. Brown's retirement date was still undetermined, so Muschamp left after the season to take the head football coaching job at the University of Florida. This wasn't the only shake-up to the staff though as Davis was forced to resign after such a poor offensive season. Davis had been Brown's assistant for 18 years, and was only year removed from directing an offense that was one of the best in the nation. Texas would definitely have a new look.

The next three seasons were better than the 5-7 year of 2010, but the high expectations that Brown had created during his tenure were unmet for Texas fans. Eight wins a year weren't enough. At the end of 2013, Mack Brown finally retired. DeLoss Dodds transitioned out of his athletic director role during the same period as well, and Steve Patterson was hired in his place. The best football job in America according to *ESPN.com* was now open, and there would be new leadership across the board.

Texas fans and alumni voiced their opinions about who should be next. Non-Longhorns often characterize Texas fans as arrogant and unrealistic. The number one person on most Texas fans' wish list fueled this fan base's description. They wanted Nick Saban, the head coach who had beaten them in 2009 and amassed four national championships at this point in his career. It was a hire they could afford and could chase with an open wallet and a great reputation. Unfortunately, not everyone concurred with the choice. Saban stayed at Alabama. Operating discreetly, Patterson went through his list of candidates and ended up focusing on the head coach at Louisville, Charlie Strong, a quietly rising star.

During 2013's coveted BCS bowl schedule, he helped lead Louisville to one of biggest upsets of the season. Louisville beat the Will Muschamp-led Florida Gators by a score of 33-23 to win the Sugar Bowl. The win put Strong on the map as a star coach. He stayed one more year and went 12-1 and won the Russell Athletic Bowl. Then Texas came calling.

Charlie Strong informed Louisville on January 5, 2014, that he would be leaving for Austin. Strong's new contract was for five years and worth $5 million per year. Texas had its new football coach, the first African American coach in its history. But not everyone shared the same enthusiasm for the hire.

"I think the whole thing is a bit sideways," said Red McCombs, one of UT's largest boosters, in an interview with ESPN 1250 San Antonio. "I don't have any doubt that Charlie is a fine coach. I think he would make a great position coach, maybe a coordinator. But I don't believe he belongs at what should be one of the three most powerful university programs in the world right now at UT-Austin. I don't think it adds up."

He added: "I think it is a kick in the face. Beyond the fact of what actually happened. We have boosters that have a lot of knowledge about the game."

The comments came off as racist and threatened to bruise UT's brand. Strong prevailed and joined Kevin Sumlin at A&M as one of two Black coaches heading the largest and most revered programs in the state. This was huge for the state of Texas, which has a history of taking its time for racial progress.

Strong took over the Longhorns team and set the tone for the program by establishing five core values: be honest, treat women with respect, no weapons, don't use drugs, and don't take something that does not belong to you. If a player challenged him and broke one of these rules, it didn't take long to see that a new sheriff was in town. Strong dismissed nine players by the time he was three games into his first season as head coach. After starting the year 1-2, criticism started to flow in.

"You have to wonder if Charlie Strong will have enough players to finish the season," tweeted *ESPN's* Trey Wingo.

By the end of his first season, Strong had formed a more disciplined, high-character team, but Texas finished 6-7 and was manhandled 31-7 by former Southwest Conference rival, Arkansas, in Houston's Texas Bowl. Strong faced more flack, but he believed in the values he was instilling. Now, he just needed to recruit talented players.

***

Uncovering the unwritten rules are crucial whenever going into a new place and establishing relationships. Texas is full of them, and failure to adhere to them can be a recipe for failure. Upon taking the job, Strong had violated an unspoken rule when he set out to Florida to recruit for the openings he still had from his upcoming class. It wasn't necessarily that Strong preferred Florida kids over Texas kids, it was that his previous job experience had given him strong connections in the Florida area. He needed players, and he needed to move fast, but in going to Florida, some felt he was overlooking Texas high school prospects. This infuriated members of the Texas High School Coaches Association (THSCA), an organization that boasts more committed members than any other national high school coaching organization in the country.

"You get here and the first thing you do is go to Florida for recruits," said South Grand Prairie head coach Brent Whitson in a *Land of 10* story. "All it did was cost him about 2,500 head coaches at Texas high schools."

Another misstep occurred at the Angelo Football Clinic, an annual summer coaching clinic that is known in football circles as one of, if not, the best clinic in Texas. If you are an invited speaker, it is crucial to publicly pay homage to the longevity and quality of the conference. Strong fell short.

"He obviously didn't want to be here," confided one coach to *ESPN's* Travis Haney. "If he did, he sure as heck didn't show it. I think everyone was shocked."

One area that Strong wanted to start focusing more recruiting efforts into was the Piney Woods of East Texas. He secured the number one recruit in the state in Mesquite's Malik Jefferson. Now, he had his sights set on the number two player, Gladewater's Daylon Mack. Mack had verbally committed to Texas A&M since he was a sophomore yet chose to re-open his recruitment after his star had climbed during his senior year. Strong's lone commitment from the

East Texas area was Gilmer's talented running back and cornerback, Kris Boyd.

Hoping to use the momentum from Boyd's signing to orchestrate a last-minute siege for Mack, Strong persuaded the young phenom to visit campus one more time leading up to his final announcement. Unfortunately, Daylon re-signed with Texas A&M, which then gave Texas A&M five commitments from the East Texas area compared to UT's one. After the disappointment of losing out on Mack, Strong decided to make staff changes. He needed to be more "Texas" and hire one of the state's premier high school coaches to his staff, so he turned his attention to Cedar Hill's Joey McGuire.

McGuire was fresh off his third state championship at Cedar Hill and was a hot commodity in coaching circles. Strong offered him the tight ends and special teams coaching position. After much deliberation, McGuire did the unexpected. He turned down the University of Texas to remain a high school coach because his son was a junior in high school, and he still dreamed of being able to coach him.

"I am staying at Cedar Hill," McGuire texted to multiple news reporters. "Most will think I am nuts, but heck, u know I am nuts. Just can't see me not coaching Garrett."

The next person Strong decided to look into was the head football coach of his star commitment, Kris Boyd—that was Jeff Traylor. At this point, Traylor was as revered as it gets in East Texas. His winning percentage was a hair above 87 percent and he had taken Gilmer to five state championship games, winning three. He produced numerous Division I college football signees and also had a handful of players in the NFL. In 15 years at the helm of Gilmer, he never had a losing season and went to the state playoffs every year with the exception of year one.

Daylon Mack officially signed with Texas A&M on February 4, 2014. On the same day, Gilmer hosted a ceremony for seven of its players who signed letters to play college football. Headlining the event one last time together were the trio of Boyd, Carter, and Lynch. Boyd signed with Texas, Carter signed with Incarnate Word, and Lynch had already enrolled at Baylor.

Six days later, Charlie Strong invited Traylor down to Austin to formally interview for the position.

"I know Charlie called Jeff," said Cari. "He didn't offer. He wanted him to interview. And that was exciting itself. He had never interviewed for a college job before. He interviewed all day. We were all at the house and our moms were there. And he did call me on his supper break, and he could only call for a brief time. And I remember the anxiety of it. You'd think that an interview couldn't possibly go that long. He didn't know for sure that night, but he had a good feeling. But until you sign the contract, you don't know."

"The University of Texas – that was his thing growing up. That's the ultimate. I think both of us were like – you can't not take it. If you get it, you have to go. If you ask him, you know he'll tell you what he went through. There was a lot of inner turmoil. To him, Gilmer was paradise. Between his family and friends and where we lived. It was his version of heaven."

After the interview, Strong extended the offer to join his staff, but even UT wasn't going to be an easy decision for Traylor. After pondering the offer as a family for five days, Traylor officially announced his decision on Twitter on February 15th.

"I have officially accepted the job at the University of Texas. I know without the coaches of East Texas none of this would have happened."

The move was widely praised throughout the state and especially in the East Texas area, but the Tweet didn't reflect the complexity of his decision. His son, Jake, and his daughter, Jaci, were both flourishing at Gilmer High School.

"I personally don't want to leave," said Traylor. "I love it here. My mother, my father, my brothers, my nephews, my nieces, and my lifetime childhood friends are all here. I feel extremely selfish for leaving, but I feel like UT is an opportunity the Lord has given me. For some reason the door is just wide open, and I think He wants me to walk through it. I've kind of felt it all year. I felt it as the season progressed. I told my closest friends and my family that I felt it."

The toughest part was leaving his family in Gilmer so that his son, Jake, could finish his senior year. That meant a 15-month separation, but he was going to be in East Texas frequently for recruiting and could see Jake's games, and he would get time in the summer to come home.

The THSCA viewed Traylor as one of their own, which was great news for Charlie Strong.

"I just believe in him (Strong)," said Traylor. "I don't think there are very many men like him left. He's old fashioned. His word is his word. He's tough. He was the biggest reason, and it's the University of Texas."

Not only did the statewide coaching association applaud Traylor's hire, but his hometown also radiated with pride. He was theirs, and they loved him.

"These people have always had my best interest at heart. They've been more than wonderful all fifteen years," Traylor said. "I have had some of the most encouraging letters and emails and texts. A lot of prayers, a lot of great people that really love me. They're the reason I don't want to go, but I feel like I need to go. I just think God wants me to go; I do, I feel that way."

Traylor was going to leave Gilmer having assembled the state's most talented coaching staff, so there was no dearth of talent for Superintendent Rick Albritton when he needed to choose Traylor's successor. On March 23rd, he recommended Matt Turner as the next head football coach and athletic director of Gilmer ISD. The man who Danny Long called "the X factor" and who Jeff Traylor repeatedly said "changed my life" would now get the opportunity to lead a program of his own. The staff, players, and community completely supported the decision. Turner was, as Todd Barr had said, "the epitome of a coach."

"Jeff will be certainly missed. We'll try to carry on. As he said, no one's bigger than the team," Turner said.

On Saturday, April 25th, 2015, in Gilmer's Civic Center, the 2014 championship Buckeye team gathered one last time for the State Championship Ring Ceremony. This year's keynote speaker was University of Texas assistant coach Jeff Traylor. More than a thousand people attended the event, even Congressman Louie Gohmert, who presented Albritton with a plaque recognizing the team's state title in this year's Congressional Record.

When it was Traylor's turn to speak, he again praised his time at his hometown school before urging the community to support Turner, who "taught me almost everything I know about coaching." It was a beautiful moment between best friends that was followed by another one when board president Jeff Rash presented a state championship ring to Darrion Pollard, Desmond's brother. The ring would proudly be displayed in Gilmer's athletic fieldhouse, and Desmond would forever be a part of the Buckeyes' story.

The last ceremonial event before both Gilmer and the University of Texas got into full swing occurred in June when Gilmer Independent School District formally renamed its football stadium from Buckeye Stadium to Jeff Traylor Stadium.

"You would be hard pressed to find a resume like that in the nation, much less in the state of Texas," Gilmer ISD board president Jeff Rash told KLTV.

"This decision is about more than wins. We've won more games than any other 4A team in the state since Jeff took over. But the primary reason is that Jeff is a hometown boy. He could have left for a lot of places in the past 15 years, but he believed in this community, and we know that he will return home one day and retire here."

Traylor called the naming the "greatest honor I have ever received."

Two of Gilmer's most loyal fans, Lena Childress and Mary Jo Dean, give a "hook 'em horns" in support of Jeff joining the University of Texas coaching staff. (Courtesy of Jeff Traylor)

Long-time assistant coach, Alan Metzel, takes over as head coach of the Buckeyes in 2020, and Gilmer advances all the way back to the 4A state championship game. (Courtesy of Ruel Felipe)

"I feel an unbelievable responsibility to do well for Texas coaches. I don't take the opportunity I've been given lightly."
--Jeff Traylor

Chapter 15: #JeffTraylorForHeadCoach

On December 18, 2020, Gilmer was back in the state championship game. Back in Jerry World. Back where they belonged. A lot had happened since their previous trip to Arlington almost six years ago to the day, for the Buckeyes and for Traylor.

Traylor's first game as a member of the UT staff was surely memorable, but for all of the wrong reasons. The Longhorns opened up on the road against Notre Dame. The Fighting Irish punished Texas in all facets of the game winning 38-3. In a game where offseason improvement is supposed to shine through, fans were left to wonder what in the heck had Texas been doing all spring, especially on offense. Strong immediately made a post-game change. Offensive coordinator, Shawn Watson, was stripped of play-calling responsibilities, and wide receivers coach Jay Norvell took over with Traylor also getting more input on the calls.

But the Longhorns saw little change and wound up losing three of its next four games before entering the annual high-stakes match-up with Oklahoma with a 1-4 record. Inspired, they shocked the country with a 24-17 win and carried their head coach off the field. The performance likely saved Strong's job as rumors were swirling around that boosters were ready to make a change. It was a bright spot in a rather dismal year. Texas finished the season 5-7, and Strong made several staff changes on offense. He was also under pressure to show that Texas could still recruit with the best of them. Traylor's star was about to rise.

Three weeks before national signing day, all of the major recruiting services ranked the Longhorns in the 30s nationally. This was a big change from the days when Mack Brown would annually haul in a top-five recruiting class. There was still time left, and Strong's top recruiter, Jeff Traylor, was championed with signing the state's top remaining player, in addition to helping recruit several others. Official visits were happening at a rapid pace, and the whole staff was collectively talking to whomever it could. It had to pull off some magic.

The number one player from East Texas, and the number one overall safety in the class of 2016, was a physical specimen out of Nacogdoches named Brandon Jones. Jones would be offered from 43 different schools. Everyone wanted him; but not everyone understood him.

"Traylor's greatest strength is relating to kids," said Steve Wells of Liberty-Eylau. "And that's big in this business."

Jones had lost his father when he was 12 years old. Traylor took the time to get to know not only Brandon, but also his four brothers. The decision would come down to either Texas or Texas A&M. Traylor's genuine connection with Jones paid off, and Jones announced on signing day that he would be coming to the University of Texas. Video footage surfaced of the entire Texas coaching staff in a meeting room erupting when Jones announced his decision. Everyone was jumping up and down except for one man. As cool as could be, Traylor sat at the conference table with his hands folded and a big smile on his face. He knew he would commit the whole time. Jones later admitted that a big part of his decision to come to Texas was his connection with Traylor.

"I just kind of listened to him and, being from East Texas, I just enjoyed what he had to say and he was very honest with me," said Jones.

Jones's decision was part of a slew of commitments. The Longhorns signing day had been unlike anything ever witnessed before, the most signing day commitments in the history of the internet recruiting age. Texas's recruiting class vaulted all the way into the top 10 nationally. It was the only Big 12 school to do so. Traylor was named the Big 12 Recruiter of the Year by *Scout*, and Charlie finally had some momentum.

***

Even without Traylor, the Buckeyes kept on winning. Now under Turner, Gilmer rolled off 14 straight wins to start the year giving them a 30-game win streak, a program record. Even more impressive was that they were now without the Carter-Lynch-Boyd trio that had captivated the entire state with their outlandish production. Players stepped up, though, especially Demarco Boyd, the 2014 Defensive MVP in the state game.

"We are really doing it for Coach Turner because this is his first year as a head coach," Demarco Boyd told KLTV. "We want him to have a good start to his career."

Turner and the staff did a marvelous job of not comparing this team to the previous season's group. They had their own identity.

"We may not have a Blake Lynch or a Kris Boyd, but we do have our team," said lineman Jake Traylor. "We have our own skill set, and we work with what we have and do our very best."

But with a larger target on their backs and a depleted lineup, Gilmer didn't punish opponents the way it had the previous year. They were finally mortal. The schedule was exactly the same as the previous year's but without lopsided scores. They beat Liberty-Eylau by five, Carthage by three, and Pleasant Grove in the first round of the playoffs by only four.

Once they got back to the semifinals, the same Celina team from the previous season was ready to get its revenge. With a trip to the state finals on the line and an opportunity for Gilmer to be back-to-back champs for the first time ever, Celina outlasted the Buckeyes by the score of 49-44.

"You've got to give [head coach] Bill Elliott and the Celina Bobcats a lot of credit," Turner told *ETSN*. "They played good football and they made a few more plays than we did."

Turner remained as classy as always. He had honorably led when his adopted community needed him.

"My kids fought their tails off and we played 48 minutes like we always say we're going to," Turner said. "We'll walk off and carry our heads high and know that we did everything we could. We shot all the bullets."

Part of what had made the program so unique for so long was the level of continuity that had remained on the staff side. When Jeff Traylor departed for the college ranks, some members of the staff pondered leading their own programs for the first time.

Shortly after Turner was announced as Gilmer's head coach, Wayne Coleman was contacted by the McCown family about coming back to Jacksonville to be its head football coach and athletic director.

"When Jeff left and the Jacksonville thing opened up, it was almost like Marshall 2.0. Do I want to stay here now that Dennis is leaving, or do I want to start over? And then you have Randy McCown calling asking me to come and coach the Indians. It was just time," said Coleman.

Coleman left in 2015, and then in the summer of 2016, Pine Tree offered its head coaching position to Kerry Lane, a 32-year-old first-time head coach. At the time, the Pirates had had only five winning seasons since 1980. It was the job that no one could figure out.

"I told them when I talked to them about the job that if all you look at is a short-term plan, you're not looking at the big picture," Lane said. "Structurally, you have to change some things to get your players excited about it and get the community excited about it. When you're trying to build something that hasn't been good in a long time, you must have different goals. I said if I was going to be selected it's an eight-year plan, not a four-year plan. It takes time to build something special."

Coaching at Gilmer was the best preparation for a task this big, but it wouldn't be easy. His old boss also warned him about replicating too much.

"When I got this job, Traylor said, 'If you try to make it Gilmer, you'll be miserable and your kids will be miserable,'" said Lane.

He recalled Traylor telling him, "Instead, think about if you want me to show up at your practice in four years, how do you want it to look? When you're used to doing it at Gilmer, you want it to look like Gilmer in a short amount of time. You'll get frustrated if it's not. Figure out what's important and get those three or four things done."

Lane and Coleman had both been transplants from other communities and had made Gilmer their home. Kurt Traylor was different. He was from Gilmer. His parents had worked at the school district, and he and his brother had built the football program from scratch. The opportunity to be a head coach had to be really attractive to get him to leave. And then, the Tyler Lee job opened.

"The previous coach resigned late, and Scott (Surratt) and Jeff (Traylor) both recommended me," said Kurt. "The AD called me up and then interviewed me for two and a half hours on the phone. Then he brought me in for an in-person interview."

"I wasn't going to take the job. I was making too much money at Gilmer. I was living on the lake. I had four kids, a swimming pool, and a dog. My mom and dad lived there. I said I'm not going to take the job unless it's the perfect job. They said, 'What's the perfect job?' I said the administration at Gilmer allowed us to do what we needed to do to be successful."

"So, sure enough, they allowed me and my staff that I brought with me to do those types of things. I got to set up teaching fields that allowed kids to be successful, and then we spent so much time on relationships with kids. I knew if I could get to their hearts, I could get to their heads, and then start driving the culture and get them to practice the way we want to practice."

All this time, the core trio of Turner, Metzel, and Barr kept the program going.

"It was different," said Metzel. "And that doesn't mean different bad. Because you had a group of people who had worked together for so long, you were just responsible for your area. You could focus on your area. When you start replacing people, the new person can be an incredible coach, but they did it differently at another school. So, all of the things we do have to be communicated and role-played."

"In some cases, coaches took three or four guys with them when they left. So, I went from the middle-aged guy to like the oldest dude in there now. Todd and I do a lot more mentoring and teaching now. I do the evaluations for the offensive side, and he did the evaluations for the defensive side. We like it though. I relish having those opportunities."

***

While the Buckeyes were going through changes, so was Jeff Traylor. Only a year after being named the Big 12's Recruiter of the Year, he was out of a job. The Longhorns again posted a 5-7 record, and Charlie Strong was fired. New head coach Tom Herman was bringing in his own staff.

"Herman sat us all down, individually," said Traylor. "He was very honest with me. He let me know that he'd like to have his own guys. But if it didn't work out, he'd reach out and let me know."

An open spot on Herman's staff never became available. Now a free agent, Traylor was highly sought out by eight different Division I programs. Only one of the schools' head coaches knew and understood how far Traylor's value could stretch out on a program though, and that was fellow East Texan and SMU head coach, Chad Morris.

Several schools from the Big 12 and the SEC made offers to Traylor, but SMU's Morris had a connection with Traylor that few could understand. Before they started coaching college football, Morris and Traylor had both been highly successful head football coaches in Texas high schools, each winning three state titles apiece. Morris knew how valuable that experience was for him not only in recruiting, but also in relating to his players effectively. The high school coach, particularly in smaller communities in Texas, is the most influential person in his or her players' lives. Morris understood that, and he knew Traylor did as well.

"If it were anybody else, I would have to prove myself to them," said Traylor. "Coach Morris and I had such a long background together. I would be walking in with immediate street-credibility again. And I just didn't want to have to go through that again. It took me a little while to gain Charlie's trust, and I wanted to be able to walk in and immediately have someone know what I was capable of."

Morris also offered Traylor the job title of associate head coach, his second in command, a role that showed the amount of respect Morris had for Traylor. Other programs craved Traylor's ability to recruit the state of Texas and utilize his relationships in a kind of mercenary role. He could find and deliver players, make no mistake about it, but Morris saw the opportunity to acquire another CEO to his staff. He knew how smart, strategic, and disciplined Traylor was in a way that others didn't mainly because Morris possessed an understanding and great respect for his East Texas bona fides.

Traylor immediately showed value in his new role, and the SMU Mustangs delivered a 7-5 season coupled with an invitation to the Frisco Bowl. It was the program's first bowl game in five years, putting Morris in high demand for open Power 5 coaching jobs.

On the morning of December 6, 2017, Morris called a team meeting for his players and staff in the film room of their football facility. The team was in the middle of finishing finals in their classes and preparing for their upcoming bowl game against Louisiana Tech, but many players had an inkling about the agenda. The previous night, news had gotten leaked on social media that their coach was in negotiations to be the next head football coach at the University of Arkansas. Bruce Feldman of Fox Sports, one of the most influential college football insiders on Twitter, even posted before the meeting at 6:15 AM that "#Arkansas has zeroed in on #SMU's Chad Morris."

This wasn't the first time Morris had been rumored to be heading to another school. The previous year it was Baylor; the previous week it had been Ole Miss and Tennessee. When a coach was as successful as Morris, these offers were only to be expected. The team was only two weeks removed from capping off its bowl-qualifying regular season with a 41-38 victory on Senior Day in SMU's Gerald Ford Stadium, and the program seemed to have some momentum. In fact, this was the first winning season in Morris's tenure. But sometimes it's easier to see statistically why this move was inevitable when you look at the numbers from SMU's last home game of 2017. Ford Stadium holds 32,000 seats. The final game at Ford, which celebrated its senior star players on the heels of achieving a bowl bid for the first time in six years, had an attendance of under 15,000. Donald Reynolds Stadium in Fayetteville, Arkansas, averages over 70,000 fans regularly, whether they're winning or not. Image is a big part of the recruiting game, and elite players want to play in an environment that is electric. Morris was ready for an easier sell.

Morris—slender and just 49 years old—walked to the podium in SMU's film room and wasted no time delivering his news to the players: he would be the next head football coach of the Arkansas Razorbacks. A dynamic speaker and motivator, he had too much respect for them to draw it out or give them phony reasons. He had built his reputation in the coaching business as being a truth-teller. He would go on to say that it was one of the hardest conversations he's ever had with a group; but in the end, he had done the most honorable thing by treating his players like men and telling them the truth. This was an opportunity he couldn't turn down for himself and his family, and his players knew it. The players also knew that this was a great opportunity for members of his staff. The salary pools of mid-major assistant coaches compared to those of Power 5 assistant coaches isn't even close. This move benefited a lot of staff members and their families, and a lot of these families had treated these players like they were members of their own household.

The reception in the room was somber yet respectful. All 118 players had shown up to the meeting, and they all hugged him afterwards. Arkansas reporter, Danny West, would later tweet that SMU players were, "sad to lose him, but happy for him." West also added that the SMU players "appreciated how he looked us in the eye." Some players even chose to recognize what Morris had done for them with a post on Twitter. SMU backup quarterback Jake Peavey tweeted, "Arkansas, y'all are getting a good one."

It was emotional for the staff, too, but there wasn't much time for reflection and nostalgia. The job change occurred during the NCAA's new early signing period for recruiting. Arkansas needed its new coach and staff to hit the ground running. When Morris left the meeting, he exited with his Director of Recruiting, Mark Smith, and they boarded a private plane to

Fayetteville. A press conference awaited them along with a new team and new recruits that needed to hear form their new head man. Other staff members would be going up soon, while some stayed back to prepare SMU for its bowl game.

Before leaving the room, Morris closed the team meeting by informing them that associate head coach Jeff Traylor would serve as the interim head football coach. That news brought some relief to an otherwise gloomy moment. While Traylor had only been on staff for a year, he was wildly popular among the players. He was also incredibly competent and could easily carry on Morris's recruiting strategy, focusing exclusively on Texas high school players and playing up his own experience as a high school coach. The strategy seemed to be working, as the program had increased its win total each year culminating with a bowl bid in 2017. With Traylor as the interim, the program could continue its upward trajectory.

Minutes after the meeting concluded, several players, led by running backs Xavier Jones and Ke'mon Freeman, took to Twitter to let the SMU athletic director, Rick Hart, know that Jeff Traylor was their choice to run the program. They even started the hashtag #JeffTraylorForHeadCoach. The hashtag was trending in the Dallas-Fort Worth area over the next five days. The support was overwhelming. This player-led movement came on the heels of the University of Oregon's football players starting a viral campaign to give assistant coach, Mario Cristobal, the job after Willie Taggart departed to Florida State. More than 70 Oregon players signed a petition to give to the athletic director, and dozens of players used the hashtag, #CristobALLIN, to garner more support for their coach through social media. The plan worked, and Cristobal was given the job. The SMU players were hoping for a similar outcome.

With a large portion of the staff already in Fayetteville recruiting for their next job, Traylor ran SMU's bowl practices with a handful of GA's and the defensive staff. SMU graduate assistant, G.J. Kinne, was one of the few members of the skeleton crew that stayed behind to help Traylor prepare the team for the bowl game. Traylor was side by side working with his old Gilmer quarterback again.

"Being interim was a blast," said Traylor. "I almost forgot how to stand as a head coach. I had to put my HC cap back on. It took me a few practices to get back into it."

During the interim period, athletic director Rick Hart received hundreds of messages of support for Traylor to be named head coach. The bulk of the messengers were other Texas high school coaches. They were rooting for one of their own.

When it was Traylor's turn to interview, the committee met with him on a Saturday evening. Sonny Dykes, the former Cal-Berkeley head coach, had met with the committee that morning. Hart let Traylor know the next day that they were going with Dykes.

"It was gut-wrenching. I thought I had the job. I was happy for Sonny though. It was a great experience. Mr. Hart was first class the entire time. The very next day I was recruiting for Arkansas. Sonny coached the team in the bowl. G.J. stayed back with him to call plays in the game. It was a great opportunity for him," said Traylor.

***

East Texas, or #bEASTtexas as it was widely referred to now, remained a hotbed of talent whose teams commanded respect across the entire state. Over the next five years, recruiting in the area continued to pick up with a record 13 players in the 2020 class being ranked in the Texas Top 100 according to 247sports.com. It also helped the interest in the area when the 2018 NFL MVP was awarded to Whitehouse native Patrick Mahomes, a three-star high school football recruit. Mahomes was evidence that there were diamonds inside the Piney Woods.

During this time, the area also won eight state championships with the signature title coming from the Longview Lobos in 2018, led by the play of quarterback and coach's son, Haynes King. It was the first time in 15 years that an East Texas school had won at the highest classification (6A), and it was the storied program's first state title in 81 years.

"They told me, 'I didn't think it would happen in my lifetime,'" Lobo head coach John King told *The Dallas Morning News*. "It put them in a different place ... knowing the Lobos truly belong as one of the premier programs."

East Texans made a practice of supporting other East Texans, and this was especially true the year Longview went to Jerry World and captured the 6A state title. The announced attendance for their game against Beaumont Westbrook was 48,421, making it the fourth largest crowd to ever watch a high school football game in Texas. By the time the game was over, the first three levels of AT&T stadium were completely full, mostly with East Texans. In a state that was becoming more urban with each passing day, the game profiled one last region of the state that still depicted Buzz Bissinger's classic literary work.

"That would be a place where you could say that it was truly *Friday Night Lights*," said Mesquite coach Mike Overton.

Of all the East Texas programs, the most outstanding one was Scott Surratt's Carthage Bulldogs. Surratt, already with four rings, captured the 2016, 2017, and 2019 state titles. His seven state championships put him at third place on the all-time list and gave him the lead among all active coaches. Simply put, he had become the best high school coach in the state.

The Gilmer family also upheld the tradition that had been established. Turner, Metzel, and Barr continued to lead the Buckeyes to at least the third round of the playoffs during each of the next four years, even in 2018 when it posted a regular season record of 4-6, but rallied to an overall 6-7 finish.

Kerry Lane led the Pine Tree Pirates to the playoffs in 2017 for the first time in 16 years and then took them again in 2019. The culmination of his work was year five when he then guided Pine Tree to a 9-2-1 record in 2020 that included a first-round playoff win. It was Pine Tree's first playoff victory since 1976.

At Tyler Lee, Kurt accomplished two things that were crucial to pleasing the community. He led them back to the playoffs, and he beat John Tyler.

"I remember the first time we played John Tyler. Danny Long calls me and said, 'Big boy, you don't know what you're about to get into. It's going to be different.' I said, 'Coach, we're 5-4 and I don't know what they are. Nobody is going to be at this game.'"

As Kurt recalled, Danny said, "'Son, it's Tyler.' I show up to Tyler Rose stadium, and it is packed out. It was one of the most intense games I've ever been a part of. Ever. And we balled out."

"Every single one of them came up to me afterwards, and said, 'Coach, I never thought we'd be able to do this. Thank you. I appreciate you helping us.' They were crying like little babies. We won state championships at Gilmer and nobody cried like this."

Meanwhile, in Jacksonville, Wayne Coleman led the Indians to back-to-back playoff appearances in 2016 and 2017, and the McCown family celebrated the retirement of their sons, Josh and Luke. When Josh announced his retirement from the NFL in *The Players' Tribune*, he made sure to also pay tribute to the greatest coach he ever played for in his storied football career, his high school quarterback coach, Matt Turner.

"There are just so many people who played huge roles in my life. Way too many people to thank here," McCown wrote. "But there is one person who I want to make sure I acknowledge, because all the success I've had in my professional life can basically be traced in one way or another back to one man. His name is Matt Turner."

"I brought his lessons with me to every quarterback room I've ever been in. His voice has been with me throughout my entire career. I see the game through his lens. He's the best coach I've ever been around and also one of the best humans. He's one of those people who you are better just for having known."

"There are just so many ways in which Coach Turner has touched my life. I'm thankful for him, and for every high school coach who makes sacrifices to invest in young people."

Of course, just a few months later, Josh came back out of retirement to play for the Philadelphia Eagles. It was his 12th NFL team.

Joining him in the NFL were Kris Boyd and Blake Lynch. Boyd had a solid career with the University of Texas, where as a senior he led them to a 10-win season and a Sugar Bowl victory over Georgia. He was then drafted in the seventh round by the Minnesota Vikings. Lynch did almost the exact same thing with his stellar career at Baylor, playing multiple positions, and eventually, helping lead the team to an 11-win season and a berth in the Sugar Bowl. While he didn't get drafted, he did get signed as a free agent by the Minnesota Vikings. The two Buckeyes were reunited.

McLane Carter ended up having a distinguished career himself. After one season at Incarnate Word, Carter transferred to Tyler Junior College where he blossomed into one of the best junior college quarterbacks in the country. Kliff Kingsbury and Texas Tech then signed him, and he spent two years being a Red Raider before joining Rutgers as a graduate transfer. Carter had always been a smart player; and after his playing career was over, he began training other young quarterbacks in Texas. His older brother G.J. also began to emerge in the coaching profession leaving Chad Morris after one year at Arkansas to briefly coach for the Philadelphia Eagles before joining the University of Hawaii as offensive coordinator.

After two tough years in Fayetteville, Chad Morris was let go by Arkansas's athletic director, Hunter Yurachek. Traylor again was left without a job. With the exception of his lone season at SMU, he had rarely tasted success on the college level. He had always delivered as a recruiter and a coach, but he was at the mercy of the jobs he took, and those jobs were all tough rebuilding gigs.

He was a candidate for the SFA head job in 2019, his alma mater, but again lost out, this time to Colby Carthel. But in December of 2019 with strong recommendations from Rick

Hart and Chad Morris, UTSA athletic director Dr. Lisa Campos took a chance on the legendary high school coach from East Texas just as he was about to interview for another head coaching opportunity.

"I remember him going to Beaumont to interview for Lamar's job, and he was driving there," said Cari. "And he found out that there was a guy who was going to interview that couldn't be there at this scheduled time, and he has to change his interview time to Sunday. So, then he had to wait a day before he'd get to do his interview. Meanwhile, he got a call from UTSA about interviewing there, and they flew him down on his off day so he'd be back in time to interview with Lamar on Sunday. And he went down and did the interview. The President was in on the interview, and I got a phone call while he was in the interview."

"He (Jeff) put me on speakerphone because the President wanted to talk to me. He asked me about what I had been doing. I told him I'd been looking at houses on Zillow. And then he asked me what I thought about the Hill Country. Anyway, he ended up sending a picture of his view by way of Jeff to show me where they live. By the time I hung up, Jeff sent me the picture, and I'm thinking he's either the nicest man in the world or the worst because he's teasing me."

At Traylor's introductory press conference for UTSA in the Alamodome, the Roadrunners' new head coach dazzled the crowd with his confidence and infectious energy.

"We look forward to being the front porch of UTSA and to the city of San Antonio," said Traylor. "I need everyone to cross that line with me and let's get this thing where it needs to be."

It was a tremendous moment not just for Traylor but also for his former staff and the town of Gilmer. Nearly the entire

Gilmer staff that worked together attended the press conference, including his old boss at Jacksonville, Danny Long. Traylor publicly thanked them all. He would soon also get two members of the old group to rejoin him at UTSA.

Only a week later, Kurt Traylor resigned from Tyler Lee to join the UTSA staff. The brothers would be working together again. It was a move that was to be expected. But then a month later, the unexpected occurred. Matt Turner retired from Gilmer. He had made the community his home for over 15 years and was now going to serve in a consultant role for Traylor and his new staff. The man who taught Traylor everything he knew about coaching was going to be back working with him in his first college head coaching job.

Again, Superintendent Albritton chose to promote an assistant from within, and the perfect candidate to keep the program on track was long-time coach Alan Metzel.

"Our program has experienced two amazing head coaches over the last 20 years and I am confident that Alan Metzel will continue to lead this program toward excellence because he has been a major part of our success during that time," Albritton told *The Gilmer Mirror*.

"All through the years you set goals as a coach," said Metzel. "It's no different than when you're a player. If you're a competitor, you want to be a head coach at some point. I've had opportunities to check into that at times, and at various times the door closed. It was just a matter of trusting that God knew the timing and place and what was best for me."

"For all these years having that desire, I was always picking people's brains. Whether it was Jeff Traylor, Mike Maddox, Jed Whitaker, Tim Russell, or Matt Turner. 'OK coach, how would you do this? How would you handle this personnel issue on your staff?' So now it's all those notes and years of preparation and it's time to go put those into action. It's time to go from theory to putting boots on the ground, and I'm excited about getting to do that."

Both first-year head coaches—Traylor and Metzel—proved to be the perfect person to lead their respective programs. In year one of their tenures, a global pandemic emerged onto the scene. Football became an after-thought as schools, workplaces, and hospitals drafted contingency plans to try and slow down the spread of the COVID-19 virus. Once permissions were given for sports to start back up, the procedures that had to be followed were necessary but burdensome. Coaches and players had to be daily tested, masks had to be worn, and quarantines had to be followed if someone tested positive. Organization and efficiency were two skill sets that were paramount for a leader during this time. Thankfully, Traylor and Metzel were steady hands that knew how to organize and lead people. The results of their actions were nothing short of extraordinary.

In Traylor's first year at UTSA, the Roadrunners won seven games and qualified for the SERVPRO First Responder Bowl. It was their first bowl invitation in four years. In the process, UTSA had a record 19 players make all-conference, and its running back, Sincere McCormick, won the *Dave Campbell's Texas Football* Texas College Player of the Year award. In typical Traylor fashion, UTSA also had the top recruiting class in Conference USA.

"The brand is hot," said Traylor.

While Traylor made it to a bowl game in his first year, all Metzel did was lead the Buckeyes back to the state championship game for the first time since 2014, this time against Scott Surratt and the Carthage Bulldogs. A new generation of players boasting some familiar last names, like the youngest son of Principal Brian Bowman, were now given the opportunity to carry on the Buckeye tradition. Carthage ended up getting the best of Gilmer, giving Surratt his eighth state championship in 13 years, but Metzel had made a statement. His team captured district over a tough Pleasant Grove program, and he did it with a young squad. They were also prepared, aggressive, and tough - just like the man who also doubled as a pastor.

"With him being so godly, you would think that he's not a guy that's going to drop the hammer on you," said Olan Johnson. "That's not the case. He's going to tell you about God, and how you should love Him and trust Him to lead you in the right direction; but at the same time, if you're not taking care of business, he's going to get on your butt; I mean, lay the hammer on you."

Gilmer had lost a lot of personnel. Todd Barr had even made the decision to retire in 2019. But the Gilmer mentality, established long ago, was that the program wins, not an individual. Former players were hired on, and emerging leaders were given more responsibility. All the while, the culture Traylor and his original staff had established continued strong. The 2020 season was evidence that what they had collectively crafted all those years ago worked. It worked in college. It worked with a new staff. And it also played an important role in helping Rick Albritton garner enough community support to finally open up a brand new, state-of-the-art high school building that solidified Gilmer as a leader in education for the East Texas area. The new building opened almost 20 years to the date after Jeff took over as head football coach. The Gilmer Way was built to last.

"One thing we always talk about is next man up," said Johnson. "We preach that with our players. One man goes down, then it's the next man up. I think Coach Metzel is doing a heck of a job."

"This place is special," added Buckeye girls coordinator Stacy Crews. "I've been under Jeff Traylor, Matt Turner, and Alan Metzel. You can't name three leaders who are more into growing coaches. You'd leave college coaching to work for them. They're the real deal."

In late July of 2021, with somewhat of a return to normalcy expected for fall football in America, a record attendance of over 10,000 coaches made their way down to San Antonio for the annual Texas High School Coaches Association's (THSCA) Convention. With Longview High School's John King as acting THSCA President, it was also Jeff Traylor and his staff's turn to be the unofficial hosts of the convention.

Traylor handled the role with his usual charm. He spoke at three different sessions, delivering the most popular one-liners of the convention to rousing applause. He and his staff then hosted a coaches' social at a popular barbecue restaurant that drew more than three times the number of people they were expecting.

"He's bigger than life," said THSCA Executive Director Joe Martin.

Not bad for a small-town East Texas coach who refined the organizational methods that originated at Judson High School, only 20 miles from where his Division I football team now plays their games (The Alamodome).

"I feel an unbelievable responsibility to do well for Texas coaches," said Traylor. "I don't take the opportunity I've been given lightly."

The Traylor family takes a picture with the Conference USA championship trophy after UTSA defeated Western Kentucky 49-41 in San Antonio's Alamodome. This was the first conference football championship in school history, and Jeff would share the accomplishment with his brother, Kurt (back row, second from the left), who had coached with him almost his entire career. (Courtesy of the Traylor family)

Epilogue

Some stories almost seem too good to be true, and this is one of them.

Jeff Traylor had just finished accomplishing one of the most remarkable feats a former high school football coach could. He had successfully transitioned to the Division I ranks, landed a college head coaching job, and led UTSA to a bowl game in year one of his tenure. High school coaches across the state of Texas, and even across the country, idolized his story. Traylor's magical ability to connect with others, regardless of background, made people see the best version of themselves in him.

High school coaches did, East Texans did, and now, even more importantly, the city of San Antonio did.

"He's the new Pop," said San Antonio resident Brandon Williams, who is also originally from Gilmer. The nickname "Pop" is a reference to Gregg Popovich, the wildly popular, long-time San Antonio Spurs coach, who won five NBA titles for the city. The Spurs last NBA championship was 2014 though, Traylor's last year at Gilmer, and the city was craving to be a winner again. The 2021 season ended up being the perfect gift.

After starting the year 10-0 and ranked in the Top 25 AP poll for the first time in program history, Traylor and his team delivered a program-defining moment when it beat UAB [University of Alabama at Birmingham], the defending conference champions, on a last second touchdown pass.

While the context was different, the moment was eerily reminiscent of Gilmer beating Tatum in year two of Traylor's tenure to give the Buckeyes their first district title in 10 years. Traylor had spoken these kinds of moments into existence within his locker rooms, and as usual, they came to fruition. This new moment put the Roadrunners of UTSA in the conference championship game for the first time ever, and due to their 11-0 record, the game would be played in San Antonio.

Two weeks later, they won UTSA's first Conference USA football championship in program history before a packed home crowd. Traylor stayed on the field taking pictures with loyal fans until the last ones left the Alamodome.

A little over a month earlier, UTSA president, Dr. Taylor Eighmy, and athletic director, Dr. Lisa Campos, had rewarded Traylor with a 10-year, $28 million contract extension. The forward-thinking offer held off larger suitors like Texas Tech and TCU from poaching their coach.

"Jeff came to UTSA with a passion for building a football program that San Antonio now calls its own," UTSA president Taylor Eighmy said. "Our team believes in him, and our students, alumni and fans are excited about the momentum. This moment in time is very special."

Never one to take trust and belief lightly, Traylor went right back to work modeling the same East Texas work ethic that had gotten him this far.

"I'm going full throttle," said Traylor. "We want this to be something that lasts forever."

Acknowledgements

Growing up in White Oak, a small town in East Texas, I don't have many memories from my childhood that don't involve going to my father's games, helping out at his practices, hanging out in the fieldhouse, or playing sports with his players or the other coaches' kids. Every day seemed to revolve around our town's high school sports teams, and the coaching staff we had was revered for the level of character by which they operated. I was raised by these coaches and their spouses, and I'm so thankful I had the good fortune to be around a staff that was so committed to the long-term success of our school and our community.

One of them, in particular, was Ron Boyett, my high school basketball coach. Coach Boyett served as White Oak's head basketball coach for 25 years, and he has had as influential of a role on my life as anyone. His unique ability to foster a lifetime attachment between his players and his basketball program is one of the primary inspirations for writing this book. I wanted people to understand why my teammates and I are so loyal to him and our other coaches, and also why we still identify as alumni of their respective programs. The time we spent under their care competing on those teams shaped us as men.

Another inspiration for writing this book was the unequivocal support of two friends, Dr. Michael Webber, the Josey Centennial Professor in Energy Resources at the University of Texas at Austin; and my University of Mississippi colleague, Professor Ralph Eubanks, himself the author of many distinguished works. Their guidance led me to eventually connect with Abigail Meisel who has become one of my most trusted collaborators. I am forever indebted to her for completely immersing herself in a story about high school football, and I'm so proud of our final result.

I also want to thank the entire Gilmer Buckeye family. When I first spoke with Jeff Traylor about this project, I was immediately given access to anything I asked for by him and his former colleagues and players. This level of generosity is unheard of when a non-member asks for insight into why a program has been successful for so long. I am so grateful, and I hope I honored their story.

Finally, I want to thank my family. My amazing wife, Brittany, has been incredibly supportive throughout this experience, and our three wonderful children, Yates, Simms, and Knox haven't known a time where I haven't been chipping away at this project, since I initially started conducting the research right before our oldest was born.

For Brittany and I, this is also a personal project. We're both from East Texas, and we both have parents, extended family, and close friends who have spent time as teachers and coaches in many of the area's school districts. I wish more people knew about their stories, because teaching and coaching in tandem is a wonderful way to make a life in a beautiful area of the country. It's a life I, myself, pursued to great satisfaction.

The Book's Coaching Tree

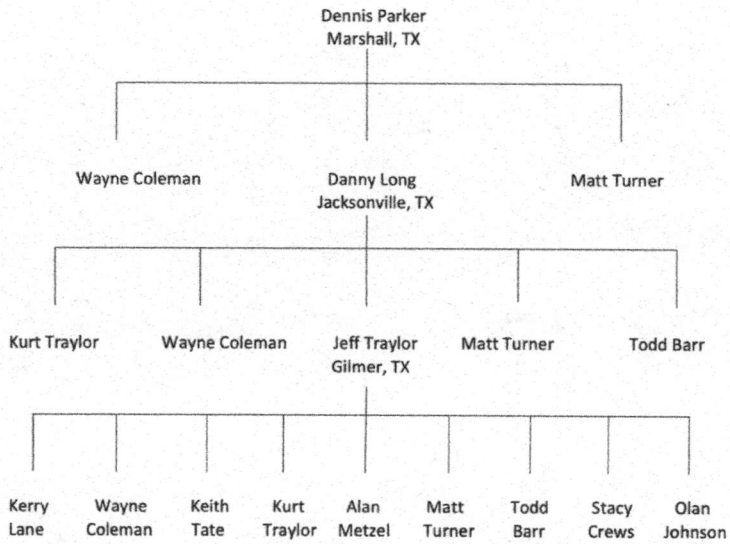

*This coaching tree graphic represents all of the coaches from Marshall, Jacksonville, and Gilmer who took part in interviews for this project or were directly quoted from other sources. I can't thank them enough.

The Gilmer Buckeyes Football Staff (2000-2014)

Barker, Craig (2000)
Barr, Todd ('00-'19)
Bennett, Will ('13-'14)
Bero, Robert ('10-'14)
Bowin, Jo Ed ('08-'13)
Black, Thad ('04-'07)
Bloyd, Doug (2000) Trainer
Bradshaw, Bill ('07-'08)
Brooks, Charles ('14-present) Maint.
Casey, Debbie ('11-'12) Trainer
Canady, Randall ('07-'14) ('21-present)
Coleman, Wayne ('07-'14)
Crawford, Joe ('00-'01)
Cunningham, Russell ('11-'18)
Edwards, Tommy ('05-present)
Eitelman, Dane ('01-'02)
Fenton, Todd ('02-present)
Gamble, Lance ('09-'11)
Gee, Bo (2007)
Grotemat, Chris (2003)
Gunter, Dustin ('11-'16)
Hagler, Nolan ('03-'13) Maint.
Hector, Joey ('01-'09)
Hedges, Trey (2001)
Henry, Lonnie ('10-'15)
Jackson, Elvis ('00-'13)
Jackson, Joey ('07-'10)
Johnson, Olan ('14-present)
Knabenshue, James ('11-'19)
Knutson, Kara ('11-'15) Trainer
King, Shannon (2001)
Lane, Kerry ('12-'15)
Langley, Burt ('05-'06)
Lovely, Terrence ('12-'14)
Low, Max ('98-present)
Loyd, Alan ('05-'07)

Maddox, Mike ('02-'05)
Marsh, Paul ('00-'06)
Mauk, Brian (2002)
Martin, Tyler (2010)
McNeel, Ronnie ('01-'03)
Metzel, Alan ('01-'03) ('06-present) *current HC
Mulkey, Steve (2004)
Pate, Phil ('00-'08) ('15-'16)
Pate, Ryan ('03-'05) ('08-'09) ('15-'17)
Potter, J.W. (2002)
Quander, Ernest (2011)
Robinson, Cody ('14-16)
Rounsaville, Mike (2008)
Russell, Tim (2009)
Tate, Keith ('98-present)
Traylor, Jeff ('00-'14) HC
Traylor, Kurt ('00-'01) ('03-'16)
Traylor, Colton ('14-'16)
Turner, Matt ('03-'19) (HC '15-'19)
Williams, Brandon (Bear) ('14-present)
Witcher, Dale (2010)
York, Steve ('01-'10) Trainer ('14-present) AAD

About the Author

Dr. Hunter A. Taylor has taught at the University of Mississippi (UM) since 2017. He is a Clinical Assistant Professor in the School of Education and an Affiliated Faculty Member in the Center for the Study of Southern Culture. He is also the Inaugural Scholar-in-Residence for the Oxford School District. In these roles, he teaches and advises administrators, teachers, coaches, and policymakers from across the state. Before joining the UM faculty, he spent 10 years as a men's basketball coach and two years as a U.S. Senate staffer.

In 2018, Taylor was named a Presidential Leadership Scholar by the Bush Institute and the Clinton Foundation for his work in education. He was one of 59 leaders chosen from across the country. He co-authored his first book, *How to Build a Thick Institution*, in January of 2022. The title comes from a TED talk that Taylor gave with Coach Chris Cutcliffe about how they improved Cutcliffe's high school football program and eventually captured the 2019 Mississippi 6A state championship. The book is a reflection on the leadership strategies the duo implemented together.